Simon & Schuster
New York   London   Toronto   Sydney

WHAT WOULD SUSIE SAY?

Bullshit Wisdom about Love, Life, and Comedy

SUSIE ESSMAN

Simon & Schuster
1230 Avenue of the Americas
New York, NY 10020

First Simon & Schuster hardcover edition October 2009

SIMON & SCHUSTER and colophon are registered trademarks
of Simon & Schuster, Inc.

For information about special discounts for bulk purchases,
please contact Simon & Schuster Special Sales at
1-866-506-1949 or business@simonandschuster.com.

The Simon & Schuster Speakers Bureau can bring authors
to your live event. For more information or to book an event,
contact the Simon and Schuster Speakers Bureau at
1-866-248-3049 or visit our website at www.simonspeakers.com.

Designed by Diane Hobbing of Snap-Haus Graphics

Manufactured in the United States of America

10 9 8 7 6 5 4 3 2 1

Library of Congress Cataloging-in-Publication Data
Essman, Susie, date.
    What would Susie say? : bullshit wisdom about love, life, and comedy /
Susie Essman.
        p. cm.
    1. Essman, Susie, date.   2. Comedians—United States—Biography.   3. Actors—
United States—Biography.   4. Conduct of life—Humor.   I. Title.
    PN2287.E755A3 2009
    792.702'8092—dc22
    [B]   2009015661

ISBN 978-1-4391-5017-7
ISBN 978-1-4391-6809-7 (ebook)

Photos for chapters 1, 2, 5, 6, 8, 9, 12, 14, and 16 by Michael Cogliantry;
photos for chapters 3, 4, 7, 10, 11, 13, and 15 courtesy of Susie Essman;
chapter 10 photo by Steve Janowitz; photos for chapters 11 and 13 by Lisa Berg

CONTENTS

For Jimmy
Who makes everything better,
and knows how to finish a basement

AUTHOR'S NOTE

When I was about nine years old, my parents had an album (I'm referring to a round piece of vinyl, which is how we used to listen to recorded music; this was a long, long time ago, even before 8-track—which is a whole other story) of Sidney Poitier reciting Plato. There was a jazz combo playing music in the background while Sidney read from Plato's writings and it all sounded like beat poetry. I had no idea what he was talking about, but I listened to it because I liked the rhythms and the sound of his voice. It was cool.

The only actual words I remember from Plato's writings were the last line of one of the pieces. I still hear it with the jazz bass plucking away under the words *"And this I know— that I know nothing."* The fact that particular line and beat have remained in my head all these years later seems significant, but when you consider that "She wore an itsy-bitsy, teeny-weeny, yellow polka-dot bikini" and "Jeremiah was a bullfrog. He was a good friend of mine" are also indelibly etched in my brain, the significance of the Plato/Sidney phrase may be diminished.

I wondered at the time, why, if he—Plato—admittedly knew nothing, did he have so much to say? Was he writing entire volumes of what he didn't know?

Now, forty-five years later, I find myself in the same predicament as Plato and Sidney. I know that I know absolutely nothing about anything—yet I have so much to say about it all. Hopefully you, the reader, will find this book – containing all the things I don't know —entertaining and perhaps illuminating. When reading it, try to imagine a jazz bass playing in the background. It might make it more memorable.

Writing this book has been a labor of love, and I couldn't have done it without the help of the following people:

Larry Amoros, my dear friend, colleague, muse and sister, thank you for your invaluable contributions. You make life funnier.

Kerri Kolen, editor extraordinaire, thanks for the smart notes, great taste, support, and encouragement from way back when.

David Rosenthal, the Grand Poohbah of Simon & Schuster, thanks for being the rabbi of this project.

Jackie Seow, for your inspired art direction, as well as Michael Cogliantry, Jeff Gautier, Chad Kincaid, Morgan Bogle, and Paul Nardi for your work on the book jacket.

Lydia Wills, my agent. Thanks for all the not-so-gentle prodding and for making this happen. Your advice was invaluable.

Gretchen Bruggeman Rush, who leaves no stone unturned when it comes to her clients' interests. Thanks for your vigilance in dotting all those *i*'s.

Lee Kernis, the *capo di tutti* of managers. Thanks for the wisdom and for always covering my back.

Oh no, the orchestra's beginning to play—my forty-five seconds of allotted time are up? But wait! I didn't thank my husband, my kids, my siblings, my mother, my friends, everyone at Simon & Schuster, anyone who ever gave me a job . . .

Shit.

The music is getting louder.

I left so many people out. Is that the *Curb Your Enthusiasm* theme they're playing? It sounds so weird with violins.

Damn it! There's the cane.

Gotta go.

Enjoy.

Susie Essman
New York City
May 31, 2009

Our heads are round so that thoughts can change direction.

—*Francis Picabia, painter and poet*

(1879–1953)

100 percent of shots you don't take don't go in.

—*Wayne Gretzky, hockey player and coach*

Kish mir en toches.

—*Millie Essman,*
forewoman in a button factory and grandma
(1898–1991)

WHAT WOULD
SUSIE SAY?

There are a number of burning questions on my mind right now: Will real estate in Manhattan rebound? Will peace in the Middle East ever be achieved? Can global warming be reversed? But by far, the most pressing question I'm grappling with is, When did I become the village idiot? How did this happen to me? How did I go from being a hip single New York City comedian with an exciting life, to being a suburban hausfrau with a finished basement and car-pool responsibilities? Easy: children. Teenagers, to be precise. Let me clarify. My new husband (how long does he stay new for? When does he become the "old" husband?—you decide, we were married in September 2008) has four children, and although technically they're not really mine, I've somehow acquired them, like they were on sale. FOUR!!!!! And three of them are girls. Oh, the drama!

They came into my life when they were ages ten, twelve, fourteen, and fifteen. Today, they are fifteen, eighteen, nineteen, and twenty-one. At least I think that's what they are. It's so confusing the numbers keep changing. Just when I've got sixteen figured out, they turn seventeen and so on. All I know is that I've been living through the "teen years" for half a decade and there seems to be no end in sight. I have this horrible fear that they'll all be sixteen forever, and I'll start looking like my grandma Millie by the end of the month.

Everything is upside down. I thought I was cool, smart, cutting edge. I'm on a hip HBO show, I work in nightclubs, I'm known for my salty tongue and irreverent point of view. Yet, now that I have teenagers, suddenly, magically, I'm an idiot. Something has gone terribly awry.

In my own teen years I was surly and sarcastic and absolutely certain I knew everything, and I mean everything. When my mother would ask/request/tell me to do something, I was more than just unresponsive or snarky—I was appalled. Was *she* telling *me* what to do? Did she honestly think she knew something I didn't? My God, she was just an adult who knew nothing and understood even less. Not to let my father off the hook, I was convinced that his sole purpose in life was to humiliate me in front of my friends, and boy, was he good at it.

Well, the joke's on me. I have become the person I used to make fun of. I am now, officially, the embarrassment.

As a teenager, I swore I'd never become my mother. Not that being my mother was so horrible, it was just that she was uncool, and in my teenage mind, uncool was the worst thing a person could be, and that includes mass murderer, proctologist, and circus clown. I was n-n-n-never going to succumb to that. But here's the humbling and shocking stuff that happens now: last year I was in the car with Cyndi, who was fourteen, driving her to her friend's house (by the way, I'm always driving them somewhere and thank God, even though I'm an embarrassment, they still let me drive them around; I don't know how my life could possibly be fulfilled if I didn't spend an entire weekend schlepping them everywhere). Anyway, Fergie came on the radio and Cyndi said, "Oh Fergie! I love Fergie!

Turn it up," and I said (totally innocently, just making conversation), "Didn't Fergie used to be in the Black Eyed Chili Peppers?" Pause. Loooooooong pause and then the ultimate sign that I did something horribly wrong—eye rolling, eye rolling, eye rolling. How do I know this is an expression of disapproval? In high school, I was queen of the eye rollers. In fact, I was so good at it, you could actually *hear* me roll my eyes. And now I was getting rolled at. Oh, the irony! Cyndi looked at me, mouth open, dumbfounded; it was a seemingly interminable moment of staggering "what-are-you-fucked-in-the-head" silence, eventually broken by gales of raucous, condescending, teenage laughter. She thought this was the funniest thing she'd ever heard and couldn't get on the phone fast enough to tell her sister what an idiot I was. (For those of you reading this who are just as stupid as moi, Fergie, and I don't mean the Dutchess of York, used to be in a band called The Black Eyed Peas. The Red Hot Chili Peppers are another group altogether. I mixed the metaphor, so to speak. She should have at least been impressed that I knew there was food involved at all.) As her laughter washed over me like a wave of obsolescence, I had this déjà vu moment, aware that this has happened before, only it was many years ago and I was the teenager and my mother was the dunce behind the wheel. She was driving me somewhere, and the radio was on and she said, "Isn't that Paul McCartney in the Rolling Stones?" Pause. Loooong pause. Eye roll, eye roll, eye roll. I gasped as though I'd caught her kicking a puppy or making out with a strange man in the parking lot of the A&P. *What a fucking idiot,* I thought. *How can she not know that Paul is a Beatle? She's so stupid!*

Now, in 2009, *I'm* the fucking idiot! Yet surprisingly, I don't care, because it turns out that with age comes perspective, and I can honestly say that I don't give a damn if I know who Fergie is or not. I like Fergie, I think she's talented, and that's all I know about her, and that's all I *need* to know about her. There is way too much information out there today about these celebrities. I resent that not only do I know who Britney Spears is and know the names of her children but that I've actually seen her vagina. It's not my fault. I didn't seek it out. I didn't break into her doctor's office, camera hidden in my lipstick, and rifle through medical files until I found the stills of Britney's bare box. The pix are on the internet for all the world to see. As was Paris Hilton's. All that money and the poor girls can't afford panties? Not that I googled Paris's pooch either. I was on the set shooting an episode of *Curb Your Enthusiasm* one day and a crowd of crew guys were gathered around a laptop, so naturally I wandered over to see what the excitement was all about. I quickly found out—there they were, on a seventeen-inch screen, the pouting popos of the pop star and the princess. While the boys in the crew seemed to be enjoying the moment, I did not need that image clogging up my brain. The internet is no place for a vagina. Imagine, these days when the gynecologist asks you to slide down on the examining table, it's so he can get a better camera angle for YouTube.

Knowing what Britney Spears's privates look like isn't cool, it's voyeuristic. When I was a teenager, we weren't watchers; we were participants, damn it! I may be an idiot for not knowing what group Fergie used to sing with, but there is no way I'm not cool. These kids and their whole lame generation think they are so hip, with their bike helmets and their safe sex. In my day safe sex was when you did it without handcuffs. We were so much wilder than they are. Cyndi went to her first rock concert when she was fourteen—Hannah Montana. She's not even a real person! The first rock concert I went to when I was her age—The Who. Hannah Montana wasn't cool last week. The Who? Still cool thirty-eight years later.

SHIT HAPPENS. Shit you never planned for and never could have imagined, and if you don't have a sense of humor about it, you're screwed. For example, I never even wanted children. When I was a kid and my friends were pretending to be mommies, I wanted to play talk show and make believe I was doing panel with Johnny. I never fantasized about my wedding or my husband or my picket fence. I always dreamed of guest hosting when Carson was on vacation.

That's not to say that having children never crossed my mind. It did. In much the same way as being a secretary, an astronaut, or a princess did. Yet at various points throughout my thirties, there were times when I would get deep physical aches to have a child, pangs that completely defied my beliefs and my vision for the future. They were intermittent, so I began tracking these pangs on the calendar, and eventually discovered that the achy-I-need-a-baby feeling always came when I was ovulating. Whew, what a relief, it was just my biological imperative rearing its head. It made perfect sense. The primordial DNA telling me, against my better judgment, that it was time for fertilization. It was what I was here for. But did I have to be a slave to my biological urges? If that were the case, then we'd all be having sex all the time, like bonobos. So the birthin' urge passed, and I was glad I didn't act on it. Besides, I didn't need children: I'd always had a dog.

Having a dog meant that I had a responsibility to another creature. It's a great human need, the desire to take care of another being. I've taken that responsibility seriously, and it has colored and limited my behavior. A child, though, was a whole other level that I was not prepared for. While much of my aversion to having a child was based on clear, rational thoughts (i.e., I'm in show business, I have a career, I travel a lot, I'm single, and I abhor both whining and drinking beverages out of sippy cups), part of it was also based on fear. My fear was that a child would take up a huge piece of my psychic energy forever. There would be a place in my brain that would never be mine again.

I'm a worrier and a merger. It's a scary world out there. How could I let a five-year-old get on the bus and go off to kindergarten? Oh, the anxiety! So much could happen, so much that I couldn't protect them from. How could I stand it if someone was mean to my kid in the playground? How could I watch their pain and humiliation? I feared that I was incapable of separating, of not making it about me.

And then there was the fear of resentment. There is a power struggle element to every parent/child relationship. According to Freud (think he rolled his eyes at *his* mother?), and I'm not sure I've got this completely correct but it's pretty close, the child always loves and hates the parent because the child is helpless and dependent and the parent has complete power over the child. And let's assume the parent uses his or her power benevolently and is only protecting the child, still, there's an inevitable power struggle, especially in the preverbal stages. I didn't want complete power over anyone. That scared the shit out of me. The least little thing you do can fuck your kid up for life. It was all too overwhelming, so I chose to remain childless. Besides, and maybe more important, there wasn't anyone who I wanted to have a child with, and although I have brave single friends who had a child on their own, I didn't want one enough to go through that, and I wasn't about to marry someone just because he seemed like a good donor.

BEFORE I met Jimmy and the kids, I was single, living in New York, relatively happy and free. Almost as happy and free as those women in the maxi-pad commercials, who are uncommonly happy and free. I was living a *Sex and the City* single woman life, except I never got laid as much as those girls. In fact, no one gets laid as much as those girls, except for gay men. Did I want to meet a great guy? Of course I did. Who doesn't want love in her life? Did I ever think the right guy would come along? I wasn't certain. Did I think he'd come with four teenagers and live one hundred and fifty miles away in the suburbs of Albany? Never in a million years.

Whatever we think we want, the unexpected is usually better. Better, but often challenging. It hasn't always been easy. When Jimmy and I first met, in 2003, we were living a two-and-a-half-hour drive away from each other. At that time, he had the kids every other week, so for the first six months, we saw each other every other weekend. I'd see the kids occasionally for dinner or something, but I never spent a lot of time with them. I didn't want to become too involved in their lives because I wasn't sure he and I would be a long-term thing. In the beginning, I thought we'd have a fling. He was hot and different, and I was very attracted to him. He wasn't in show business and didn't know anything about my world, which was charming and refreshing. About three months into our relationship, Jimmy traveled with me to a gig for the first time. We went to HBO's Comedy Arts Festival in Aspen, where I was performing. There were tons of people there I knew—comedians, agents, managers, network executives. It's a big scene. I was a little nervous about how this rube from upstate would fit in. The first night we were at the very noisy bar of the hotel, where everyone congregates. I introduced Jimmy to Chris Rock, and Jimmy leaned in and said, "I'm sorry, what's your name, Mark?" I loved it. He had no idea who anyone was unless they were sports figures. The only time I ever saw him impressed, was when I introduced him to John McEnroe. It was great. And everyone loved him because he was so natural and guileless. He was a guy. No pretense. No bullshit. And on top of that, he was fun and warm and real, but the physical distance between us and the circumstances of our lives seemed like a lot to deal with. I was certainly not interested in becoming a "stepmother." That was the last thing on my mind. I was a career girl.

So, naturally, we fell in love. What started as fun turned into forever; I was looking for lust and got love. After about six months of dating I knew it was time to take the plunge and spend a weekend upstate when he had the kids. That was daunting. First off, I don't know much about upstate New York. For most people in Manhattan, anything above Yankee Stadium is "upstate." Secondly, it meant that I'd be living with four adolescents all weekend. To me, this was a big thing. Jimmy, as is his way, thought nothing of it.

Truth be told, I was scared of the kids. Ah, *fear,* the "F" word again. I didn't know how to talk to them or be with them. Jimmy is so easy and natural with his children. I was used to being alone with him, not sharing his attention with anyone else, but I knew enough to accept the fact that they came first and not compete. It wasn't easy. I'd never been in a situation like this before. All of my previous boyfriends had been childless. One had had a dog but that was about it.

The only experience I could draw on was being an aunt. I was always Auntie Mame to my nephews. I doted on and adored them. I took them to shows and ball games, and showered them with gifts for an afternoon or sometimes a sleepover. Then I sent them home to their parents. I love being an aunt. It's rewarding and effortless.

I spoiled my nephews and they seemed to like it, so I figured why not buy Jimmy's kids' love? I know, you're thinking, *That's despicable.* Think again, it worked like a charm.

My mother tried to give me advice. She'd say, "You know, you can't buy their love." Bullshit. You can, and it's exponential. They're like Russian mail-order brides—the more you spend, the more they love you. They're teenagers! It's all about things! Besides, shopping was the only thing I knew how to do with them. They were all athletic and I'm not in the least, so I'd show up on the weekend and Jimmy would suggest tennis or skiing and I'd say, "Okay kids, let's go buy stuff!" and they'd follow me like I was the Pied Piper.

They loved it, and so did I. I'm really good at it too. I'm stealthy. I'd show up Friday night, hit 'em hard, and then by Monday morning, I was out. It was great. I was part of the solution, and it all worked beautifully. I'm shallow and they were even shallower.

That's not to say that all I did was spend, spend, spend. It really wasn't that calculated and subversive. It was more sub-conscious. There was a lot that was difficult, but these kids were really so incredible. Luckily, I fell in love with them be-fore I ran out of money. One of the things you can't buy is time, and one day, I don't know exactly when, I started to feel more comfortable and started taking to this stepmom thing like a fish to water.

Now I don't even think about whether or not I want to be a parent. I just am. I'm not their mother. They have a mother and they have a father. For a long time I was their father's girl-friend and somewhere along the way, before Jimmy and I got married, the kids began referring to me as their stepmother and I to them as my stepchildren. Our relationship had be-come more than "my Dad's girlfriend" implied.

I can say, *"I love them as though they were my own children,"* but I don't have my own children so I don't know if that's true. I do love them unconditionally and without expecting anything in return, and if that's what parental love means, then I've got that covered. The loving part is not difficult, but frequently the parenting part is. Who wants to be a disciplinarian and sometime bad guy? That was never a part of the Auntie Mame scenario. At least, in all the fights I've had with them—and I've fought with each and every one of them at one time or another—none of them ever screamed, *"You're not my mother!"*

I think they trust that I have no agenda with them beyond my responsibility to protect and care for them. Since I met them when they were a bit older, I can see who they are as individuals without any preconceived notions, and hopefully I can help them navigate the difficult adolescent years. And just as I feared and suspected, a piece of my psychic energy has been lost to me forever. I worry about them all the time and with good reason. They're teenagers.

When I first began to spend time with them, I thought it would be a good idea to find out why teenagers act the way they do. Why do they have really poor judgment and no sense of long-term consequences? How come they have no organizational skills, and why do they have poor impulse control? Why are they so susceptible to peer pressure? And did I mention that they think they know everything (and I mean everything)? Sound familiar? I remember it all too clearly.

❇   ❇   ❇

I DID some research on the teenage brain and learned that the cerebral frontal cortex is not fully formed until the age of twenty-five. Which means that teenagers are mentally ill and you've got to assume that they're partially brain damaged until they're in their midtwenties! That's a long time. My youngest is fifteen! Even if they're responsible and great kids, and by and large mine are, they're still impaired, and it's not fair to them to assume otherwise. Right now, all four of them are mentally, hormonally, and neurologically imbalanced creatures—imbalanced creatures with car keys.

Oh, and by the way, they lie, each and every one of them, instinctively and almost pathologically. What kills me the most is that they think we don't know they're lying—and they're not even that good at it! Do I look like a freaking idiot?

Here's how it works: They lie, and they know they're lying, and we know they're lying, and they suspect that we know they're lying and nobody says anything. It's like dealing with Dick Cheney! So we ask a lot of questions.

"Where are you going?"

"Out."

"Out where?"

"I don't know, we haven't decided yet." (Which is teenage speak for "we don't know whose parents aren't going to be home yet.")

"Then you can't go."

"Alex's house."

"Who's going to be there?"

"Everyone."

"Are Alex's parents home?"

"Yes. Why do you always ask me that? You're so annoying!" (Eye roll, eye roll, eye roll.)

Everyone's always going and the parents are always home. And apparently my kids are the only ones who have to be home at midnight. According to my kids, all the other kids have a curfew sometime this coming October. We are so strict!

"Courtney's mother always lets her go."

"Well, if Courtney was my kid, I'd let her go too. She's a horrible child. Her parents don't want her to come back. Who's driving?"

"Mike is. He's a really good driver."

"Good driver? He got his license last week!"

"That doesn't mean he's not a good driver. God, you think you know everything!" (Eye roll, eye roll, eye roll.)

You people with younger children or no children at all may be getting judgmental and thinking, *You should call and speak to the parents, etc. etc.* It's not so easy. There are so many of them, and do you know what it's like having conversations with some of these parents? And besides, sometimes you've just got to trust your kids. For example, when my girls tell me they're not having sex (and yes, I ask), I believe them, even though I know they're possibly lying. No parent really wants to know their daughters are having sex, so we pretend, even in the face of overwhelming evidence, that they're not—until one day the delusion is ruined when the little darlings get flowers from the New York Knicks. It's not pretty. Maybe I really am an idiot. When you've got teenagers, denial is a beautiful and necessary thing.

※　　※　　※

PEOPLE ALWAYS ask me what it's like to live with all these kids. I tell them I live my life in fear. My mother laughs. She's thinking "payback" (and enjoying it a little too much). I think of my teenage self. I think of all the stupid things I did, teenage things, life-threatening things. I had "teenagethink," as in, Nothing is ever going to happen to me, I'm immortal. I thought I knew everything and was so much smarter than my idiot parents.

I lie awake at night and think about how to protect the kids from themselves. They're still children no matter how mature they think they are. They're caught in a weird netherworld between *The Wizards of Waverly Place* and *Gossip Girl.*

How do I keep them safe in this unsafe world? How do I keep my mouth shut when I know they've got a bad friend? So often I know what will make them happy, yet I have to stand by helplessly and watch as they make wrong choices, knowing that they've got to figure these things out for themselves. How can I teach my stepson to be a strong man but not a macho asshole? How can I explain that promiscuity is not a good thing but, at the same time, his sexual desires and interests are healthy and normal? And with the girls, how can I warn them that there are creepy men in the world who will do harm to them if they're not vigilant and at the same time convey to them that they can trust men and have meaningful relationships with them? How can I get them to stop dressing so provocatively without making them feel ashamed of their bodies? It's challenging.

There are no clear-cut answers. We do the best we can. We try to be good role models, but there is so much that is out of our control. We try to instill values and morals and eth-ics. We try to do the right things. Jimmy finished the base-ment so they'd have a place to hang with their friends and not have to drive around with someone who's been drinking or smoking. Keep them close to home. It was a good plan. But at 3:00 a.m. on a sleepless night I think, *How many teen-age pregnancies have been conceived in newly renovated base-ments?* And by 4:00 a.m. I'm thinking something even worse. *What has become of me—hip, cool, cutting-edge New York City comedian—that I even have a renovated basement?* (Eye roll, eye roll, eye roll!)

CHAPTER
2

GAY—NOT GAY—
SHOULD BE GAY

There was a time (when I was single and unattached) that I prayed for lesbianism to strike me. I'd dated all kinds of men—young men, old men, short men, tall men, handsome, not so handsome. . . . It became exhausting. I went on thousands of dates. How many times could I say, "Don't be silly, accounting *is* fascinating," or "No, please, I *do* want to hear more about your mother." Even though I lived in New York City, a town with three million males living within its borders, I was convinced that I would never find a straight man who wasn't (a) dull, (b) very dull, (c) narcissistic, or (d) narcissistic and dull. I felt I had no recourse and lesbianism was in the offing. But it never happened. Actually, it never even got off the ground . . . or, should I say, carpet? I am who I am, and as much as I loved my girlfriends to hang with and talk to, I didn't love them in *that* way. I can barely swim, let alone dive.

I had this notion that since it's so much easier to become friends with women than hetero men, why not kill two birds with one stone and just have women as my love objects as well? On paper, it made perfect sense. As a rule, I find women far more fascinating than men, and not just because I am a woman but because men are kind of simple and women are complex. Women have a sophisticated biological infrastructure, uterus, and ovaries, fallopian tubes, and whatnot. We've got major goings-on down there, and it's pretty incredible.

We're capable of creating an entire human being inside our bodies. How many people can say that, huh? Women can, that's who.

Men have a protrusion. It's really simple. It either works or it doesn't—the possibility of which occupies most man's every waking thought. "Is it going to work today? It worked yesterday, but how can I be sure it will work again on Tuesday? Or Friday? Or in October? Is it as big as his? Bigger? Biggest?"

Straight men are consumed with the size of their units. They treat them like real estate—a high rise or a low rise, is it expandable, a junior four, what's the square footage? Men are far more concerned with size than women are. This is not to say we don't care, we do. It just doesn't have to be some massive, gargantuan freakish kind of thing. I personally don't want to see a penis so gigantic that when it approaches I have to get my affairs in order and notify my next of kin. On the other hand, no woman really wants to go to bed with a guy and repeatedly ask, "Is it in yet?" What's the point? It's like going to one of those nouvelle cuisine restaurants where the portions are so small, when you get home you have to feed yourself again. Why not just save the aggravation, stay in, and raid the fridge?

The truth is, most of you guys are just fine, yet all men—big or small—desperately need you to tell them it's huge. If you do that with even a modicum of sincerity, they'll be happy. You won't even have to worry if what you're doing is good; they won't care, because men don't have a G-spot. Did you know that? Isn't that weird? You can put their manhood through a meat grinder, but as long as you keep telling them how big it is, they're fine. "Oh my God, it's huge. It's the biggest thing I've ever seen. What do you feed it? Geez, put that thing on a leash! It's gigantic. I'm scared. I am physically afraid of that thing. It's so big, I'll never be able to access it!"

IT'S AMAZING how easy it is to please a man.

Men start wars over this stuff. They do. If all penises were manufactured at a plant in Detroit somewhere and they were all the same size and they all always worked—well, then they'd have to be manufactured in Japan—but anyway, if they were all the same, war would be virtually unheard of. I'm completely convinced of that. I'll bet you that a lot of wars started by U.S. presidents can be traced back to the Washington Monument. Here's how it works: a president comes into office feeling pretty good. He just won an election, he got millions of votes, he kicked the other guy's ass, everybody wants to be his friend and have a sleepover. Then he takes office and realizes how powerless and lonely and isolated he really is, and in the midst of all this ennui, every day he looks out the window and sees the Washington Monument, this huge phallic symbol looming over him, and he begins to feel more and more inadequate and small and meaningless and impotent, and finally, he goes and invades some country so he can feel better about himself. As I said, it's pretty simple. It's all about the penis, all the time. Women are nowhere near as genitally focused. Men do things like expose themselves and masturbate in public. What is that? It's disgusting! I've seen it way too many times for it to be anecdotal. You never hear of a woman fingering herself in the Walmart parking lot, do you? End of story.

Years ago, when I was struggling with the male/female dilemma, I read the book *Men Are from Mars, Women Are from Venus.* Although the self-help-book genre was not my cup of tea, I found this one to be astute and enlightening. The entire premise of the book seemed to be that men are emotionally retarded and women have to understand just how emotionally retarded men are and make allowances for their retardation. According to the book, when men are confronted with emotions, they go into a cave and don't want to talk. Then they "rubber band" or some *mishegas,* where they come close, then snap back. It all sounded so infantile and accurate.

The book also says that the major differences between men and women are not as much their genitals as their mouths. Men use theirs to eat or mumble or burp, women use theirs to (horror of horrors) talk, communicate, and exchange thoughts and ideas and feelings and feelings and feelings and feelings. The very thing that separates us from our simian ancestors is the gift of speech, and women choose to use that ability to full effect. Men choose simply to drag their knuckles. Maybe the book should have been called *Men Are from Hunger, Women Are from New Jersey.*

Just to clarify this talking thing, I do know many straight men who like to talk, but sadly, that's the problem. It's not the talking per se, it's the content. They'll talk, but not about anything particularly interesting. My father, for example, could talk endlessly about himself (a subject he never got tired of), regardless of the mustard-gas-like effect his chatter was having on everyone else in the room. My husband is also a talker. He's not of the egotistical order, but Jimmy will go on and on about every little detail of some commercial real estate deal he's working on. I love that he's so into his work and that he loves me enough to think I actually give a damn about the story he's telling, but he gives way, way, way too many details. He talks about blueprints and loading docks and escrows . . . the stuff of which mass suicides are made. I can deal with it now that I've figured out how to let him know that what he's saying is just slightly less torturous than water boarding. I've got a code word for him. I listen and try to be attentive, but when it reaches the point where the blood starts draining from my head and I begin to lose consciousness, I simply scream, "GLAZING!" Which is shorthand for, my eyes are glazing over, which is shorthand for, "You're boring the shit out of me, finish the goddamned story already!"

I'm a comedian. I live for the punch line. A story that Jimmy spends fifteen minutes telling could easily be told to hilarious effect in ninety seconds or less. Give the salient points, punch it, and done, on to the next story. You're in, you're out, ba-da-bum! Kind of like some guys I've dated.

Still, there are a lot of great things about straight guys. If you accept them with all their limitations, foibles, insecurities, and nose hair, you will frequently be pleasantly surprised. Jimmy, for example, finished the basement in our house. I'm not kidding, he did it all by himself and it's gorgeous. He'd be down there for days and days working with his tool belt on, so focused, and it was hot. True, there are lesbians that could have done the same, but that would never have worked its magic on me in the same way. That's why if you're a woman who's sexually attracted to men, then you better figure out how to deal with them or you'll be miserable. I think the trick is not to expect them to be anything like your girlfriends, your gay friends, or even your family pet. Thinking your man is going to give a shit about the minutiae that your girlfriend has the patience to listen to is the kiss of death. And if that's all you're looking for, then I suggest we return to the concept of lesbianism as an alternative.

It turned out to not be an option for me. I love men and seem to be tragically heterosexual, but I'm just one woman—don't necessarily rule it out for yourself. Know the pitfalls, though. For example, there's the notorious and well-documented lesbian bed death. That's when about three weeks into a relationship the sex goes and is replaced by total and complete focus on their cats. For some inexplicable reason, about twenty-one days into a romance, lesbians begin obsessing about the wrong pussy. Also, they take the talking thing to a whole new level. When two women are in an intimate relationship, they talk about their feelings endlessly. This makes a grunt here and there during a football game sound very appealing.

And, lesbians never really break up. They stay connected to each other years after the relationship is over, so when you're in a lesbian relationship you've got to spend all your holidays and free time with their exes. For many years, I was convinced that there were only fourteen lesbians in the whole world and that they'd all dated one another and kind of rotated around, and once a month they all got together to have a cup of Earl Grey and listen to Dusty Springfield albums.

Even considering the pitfalls, I'm very fond of lesbians in general and still regret that I'm not one. They always seem confident and happy and secure in their Sapphic enclaves, and they're always decent and upright citizens. Be honest, when was the last time you heard of a lesbian counterfeiter or numbers runner?

I think lesbians get a bad rap for not being as fabulous as gay men. I know many a fabulous lesbian who dresses great and has taste and style. They don't all have platinum cards at Home Depot. In fact, I hereby do declare that lesbians are the new gay men, because lately, so many gay men seem to be having identity crises. Let me explain. Gay men are the most fabulous creatures on earth. They have style, flair, and can be in a long-term committed relationship and still sleep with whomever they want whenever they want. How hip and enlightened is that? As a hetero woman, I could never in a million years accept that, but gay guys, like many men, are able to separate sex from love and see it for what it really is—sex.

Gay guys are not as touchy about this stuff as heteros. They know that ultimately, compatibility is about smell. That's right, smell. There are five senses (six, if you count "fashion"), but smell is the big one when it comes to sex. Did you know that women with sinus trouble are three hundred times more likely to be single than other women? Of course you didn't; I made that up, but I'm trying to make a point here. To this day, I can conjure up the smell of every boyfriend I've ever had. Once, I stayed with a guy for three years because his scent reminded me of a long-lost love. The first time I met him I practically smelled him across a crowded room, and I had to have him. Sometimes in the cold he would smell exactly like the ex and I would get confused. I'd smell him the minute he walked through the door, and I wouldn't wash the pillow he'd slept on so I could smell him when he wasn't there. Another guy I went out with had no scent whatsoever. I'd smell his clothes when he wasn't looking. He left a coat in my closet, and I'd sniff it endlessly trying to find a trace of him, but I never found it. It was like dating a cyborg. The relationship didn't last long.

It can work the other way around as well. I ran into an ex-boyfriend a few weeks after we had broken up, and I was repulsed by his scent. So much so that a wave of nausea came over me and I felt faint. How could my nose have betrayed me, or more to the point, how could I have betrayed my nose?

When I walk my dog and another dog comes over and they start doing the sniff dance, they either like the way the other one smells or they don't. And dogs remember one another's scents forever. When a dog sniffs a fire hydrant, he can know everything about every dog that's ever peed there, yet a suburban housewife whose husband has buried bodies under the house never seems to notice anything. Strange, no? Anyway, if dogs don't want to play and are not attracted to the scent, they walk away and no one's feelings are hurt and no one feels rejected. Humans take all that stuff to heart. But the truth is, we're either sexually attracted to one another or not and there is no forcing it. Maybe the human scent thing has to do with picking the person that has compatible genes to procreate with. I don't know. But I do know that it's as important to listen to your nose as your gut and the two may be inexplicably linked. If a guy doesn't smell right, then the odds are you're not sexually compatible and he's not for you.

Gay guys get the whole attraction and compatibility thing. They get that it can't be forced and it is what it is. A top is a top, a bottom is a bottom, and some are both but you can't fit a square peg into a round hole. Heteros go through all sorts of machinations about sex and when to actually have it. Gay men don't seem to do all that. I have a gay friend who has sex on the first date before he and the new beau even go out to dinner. That way, if the sex is bad, why bother with the formality and expense of a meal? Saves lots of time and heartache and leaves more of your credit line available for shopping and theater tickets.

Growing up, I never got good advice from my elders about these things. Instead I'd hear ridiculous stuff like, "Why buy the cow when you can get the milk for free?" Translation: if you have premarital sex, he'll have no reason to marry you. Well, that was fine with me. Who says I wanted to marry him? Besides, since when am I a cow? Not only am I not a cow, I'm lactose intolerant! And do you really want to be bought? Don't forget that once owned, you have no choice but to give the milk whether you're in the mood or not.

If you're going to have sex with a man before you marry him, and who isn't (even those "abstinence only" Palin girls seem to get busy before getting married), then at what point in the relationship do you do it? This is a complicated question. That whole he-won't-respect-you-if-you-give-it-up-too-soon concept really pisses me off. How come he's never worried if we'll still love him in the morning? It's the old Madonna/Whore trap. If you're the Whore, well then, you're the Whore, and if you're the Madonna, you'll never have a good time with him in bed. He may be having a grand old time, but you're stuck with his fantasy. Either you'll feel inadequate and worry that he's off, with the Whore getting his rocks off, or you'll try to perk up your own sex life, which will never work because the minute you start to indicate that you actually like sex, he'll need a prescription for Cialis.

The most compelling reason for waiting to have sex with a guy is that, as I've said, men are simple. Women have to understand men's simple needs. One of them is that men have to be the pursuers. Remember, they're the ones that have to get the erection, not us, and nothing gets them so hot as the chase. This applies to the relationship as a whole and not just the sex. In the beginning, the girl may have to make the first move and let the guy know she's interested, because remember, guys are deeply insecure and afraid of rejection and have to know that they will be well received, but after the girl's initial nudge—she's given him the cue and he's picked up on it—then it's his job to pursue. He's the hunter, and if he's pursued, chances are he'll run the other way.

After the first time I met Jimmy and he had my phone number, he didn't call for two weeks. Claimed he was busy. Busy? For two weeks? Barack Obama isn't that busy, and he's running the country! So, I called him first and broke the ice and gave him encouragement. After that, I didn't initiate a call for six months. He'd call and leave messages, and I'd just let him call again until he got me. I was responsive, but not too readily available. A game? Of course! That's the whole point. Part of the fun of the dance is figuring out the choreography.

I know, this still doesn't answer the question of when to have sex with a guy. I don't know if there is an answer. First date? Tenth date? Six months later? I have one friend with OCD who says you should only have sex with the guy on Tuesday at 7:43 p.m. central standard time, but she may not be the best one to put the question to. Some of my friends say you should sleep with him right away because you've got to find out immediately, if not sooner, if the sex is good. Bad sex, by the way, is a concept that most men can't fathom, because they'll stick it in anywhere and they're happy, but for women, there is definitely such a thing as bad sex—the kind of sex where you're thinking, *Can you get into a marginally erogenous zone?* And meanwhile he's got his penis in your eye socket! What if you really like the guy, and you wait and wait and wait, and then you finally sleep with him and the sex sucks? You try to talk yourself into the fact that it's not that bad and it'll get better. Trust me, **it won't get better.** Men never know they're bad in bed. Even when you tell them point-blank, repeatedly, *loudly,* and with vigor and gusto, they will refuse to hear you. Then you're forced to break up with him and hurt his feelings and you're all emotionally involved already. It's not fun. I mean, maybe you're in love with the guy and then find out he sucks in bed. Do you leave him for that? It's kind of superficial, but what are you supposed to do? Stay and end up having an affair with the plumber? It's so disappointing. Who needs it?

So I say sooner rather than later, although I'm not advocating promiscuity. I'm not talking about hooking up with a guy you met in a bar. I've never regretted anyone I *haven't* slept with, but there's got to be some happy medium. If you're dating someone and know you're going to sleep with the guy eventually (and sometimes you just know), you might as well just do it—with adequate protection, I might add. If the sex sucks, then look on the bright side: no wasted time telling him your deep, dark secrets, no worrying about his ex-girlfriends or what he thinks of you naked or whether he's going to call the next day or not or if there's something wrong with you.

It's not that relationships are only about sex, but if the sex isn't there, especially in the beginning, then I'm not really interested. I was once told that sex only takes up 3 percent of the time in a married couple's life, so the other 97 percent better be good. But if that 3 percent sucks, then why stay in the first place? Why not just opt for the lesbian bed death?

Sadly, it seems that these days, that's what a lot of gay men are doing. Gay guys who were so forward-thinking about sex and style are now blowing it! Or not blowing it as seems to be the case, because all these great gay guys want to get married and adopt children and move to Montfuckingclair, New Jersey! They want to be like *them*. Those people at the mall . . . those overburdened and overdrawn desperate housewives and their pasty, whipped husbands who sit at the food court stuffing their faces holding shopping bags while they wait patiently for their wives to come out of whatever midrange shoe store they've been sucked into . . . the June and Ward Cleavers of the world! And there's nothing wrong with those suburban couples at the mall, but we already have enough of them. More than enough.

We need gay men to be gay men! We need their taste and joi de vivre and bitchiness and warmth and style and sense of fun and humor and sexuality and friendship and color. But since they're so ready to give up their birthrights as the greatest and most talented species on earth, then I think it's only fitting that lesbians, who as a group have been maligned as having no talents or style, should be anointed the new gay men. Gay men are now the new soccer moms, and soccer moms are the new lesbians. If the Birkenstock fits . . .

I have a house in the suburbs and I go to the soccer and soft-ball games, and these moms—besides being ridiculously and dangerously overinvolved with their kids' teams—have com-pletely given up their sexuality. They're wearing aluminum siding. They're using their wombs to store the kids' winter clothes. If you drop any of these women and their bad mullet haircuts down in the middle of Provincetown, they will fit right in. What has caused all of these lovely suburban couples to become asexual parenting machines is something else I've studied (think I have too much time on my hands?), and I have a theory (surprise, surprise!): I believe that the main reason the sexuality of these suburban couples has gone bye-bye is that the husbands were in the delivery room when their wives gave birth. Like animal testing and offshore drilling, this is a practice I strongly oppose. Call me old-fashioned, but I pre-fer the days when the expectant father was out in the wait-ing room, smoking a cigar and pacing. I think that's far better for the maintenance of a healthy sexual relationship. Men are such visual creatures, and once they actually watch the birth of their child, it becomes, forever, a whole other vagina to them. When you go to a great restaurant, you don't want to see what goes on in the kitchen, do you? Besides, when men see an eleven-pound baby coming out of there, they begin to feel pretty damn inadequate, pretty damn fast. For the father it was a place for sex, for the kid it was housing. And yet, hours later, with the wife healed and the husband resuscitated, the couple, not yet aware that their sex life was, at least as they knew it, over, always say that it was a great experience and it was so "personal." You know what? So is taking a dump, and I don't want my husband or anyone else watching that.

Okay, then let's review: lesbians are the new gay men and gay men are the new soccer moms and soccer moms are the new lesbians. That leaves us with only one more group, the "should be gay" contingency. Those men and women who, by all physical, behavioral, and attitudinal standards, *should* be homosexual: the ultra-faggy dad, the unreasonably "handy mom." This is a weird group, because through years of having to be both sensitive and outrageous, soft yet strong, they are in constant conflict with themselves and the world around them. You know the ones, the guys you meet and you assume they're gay and then they mention the wife and kids. You try to muffle the laugh, or retard the expression of shock that crosses your face, as though you'd just been told that Paris Hilton was starring in a revival of *Agnes of God* on Broadway.

There seem to be a lot of these "Are you suuurrre they're straight?" types in Hollywood. They say that if you walk into a guy's office and the pictures of his wife and kids are facing in, toward him, then he's straight, but if the pictures are facing out, then he may be gay. I think that if you walk into a guy's office and the pictures of his wife and kids are facing the pictures of Brad Pitt and Mario López, then he's definitely gay.

I have a number of friends who have left their wives and come out recently. They're always shocked that you're not shocked when they tell you. As though we had no idea all along. Everyone knew. Strangers knew. I knew at the wedding! It's like nobody told them that they're supposed to be gay. Well, I'm here to tell them that they are. If you're a man and you're mucho feminito, then go out, suck a dick, and get on with it. Likewise for the butch girl (except without the blow job, obviously).

I know, I know—I'm unfairly stereotyping. Just because a woman looks like a high-school gym teacher doesn't mean . . . but yeah, it usually does. Sex, gender, desire, conditioning, it's all so mercurial and you never know what's around the corner. It is what it is, and trying to change it is really futile and stupid. If one day one of my daughters comes to me and tells me that lesbianism has struck, well, I'll be oh so happy to invite her girlfriend and girlfriend's exes and her girlfriend's exes' cats into our family forever and ever and ever and ever.

A FEW CLUES THAT YOUR HUSBAND MIGHT BE GAY

You make him a hearty, all-American dinner, and over dessert he says that the meat loaf was "decadent and thrilling."

He spends an inordinate amount of time worrying about pillow shams.

He knows what pillow shams are.

He has a lifetime subscription to *Men's Health*—even though he's five foot nine, weighs two hundred and forty pounds, and hasn't seen the inside of a gym since high school.

He owns five cats, all named for characters in Barbara Stanwyck movies.

At the mall, he's much too eager to hold your purse while you pop into Lane Bryant.

He's rolled his eyes and said, "Whatever" on at least three occasions.

In the last presidential election, he cast a write-in ballot for Matthew McConaughey.

When watching NASCAR events, every time the TV announcer says "horsepower," he gets all flushed and giggles.

You caught him in the garage blowing your neighbor.

He's reading this book.

CHAPTER

3

SIT! STAY! ON SECOND THOUGHT, MAYBE YOU SHOULD GO

Sumo Essman-Harder

I come home late at night, and there he is, in the bedroom, lights down low, on the bed, on his back, licking himself. No, no! Not my husband. My dog!

I love dogs. I'm dogcentric. A dogophile, some would say. A dog can't pass me in the street without catching my eye and making me fall in love. I've never seen an ugly dog. I think each and every one of them, no matter their breed or size, is absolutely adorable. They make me laugh, they make me cry, and I feel a responsibility to make the world a better place for them—millions of fire hydrants, biscuits galore, premium cable . . . whatever they want, whatever they need. I'm there to give. I've always had dogs. My current little guy, Sumo (he came with that name), is a rescue. He was five when I got him and he's just the greatest.

I've had him for four years now and I tell myself that he knows he's a rescue and that he's undyingly grateful to me for saving his life. I also like to believe that he enjoys light opera, loves distressed wood furniture, and thinks that Norman Mailer was sadly misunderstood. Odds are I'm fooling myself and all he really cares about is food.

On the one hand, dogs are really incredible creatures capable of doing amazing things. There are countless stories of dogs saving people's lives or traveling thousands of miles to find their masters or staying by your side when you're sick, etc. And what about those incredible dogs that help the blind and infirm? They're just remarkable. Did you know that a companion dog is able to tell an epileptic that a seizure is coming up to forty-five minutes before it actually happens? It's amazing when I consider that a couple of my ex-boyfriends weren't able to give me a forty-five-second warning before they were coming.

And then on the other hand (and there's always another hand, isn't there?), dogs are the most manipulative creatures on earth. They could make Marie Antoinette seem altruistic. Why do you think they're so cute? It's so they can wrap you around their furry little paw. I don't really know if my dog loves me or if he is just really good at getting what he wants. But if we're anthropomorphizing them in order to believe that we're receiving unconditional love, is that such a bad thing? And does it even matter? If I feel loved, isn't that more important than whether that love is real or imagined?

No one has ever been as happy to see me walk through the front door as my dog. But is he happy to see me because of undying affection, or is he happy because he knows I have the keys to his ultimate happiness, which is, of course, the key to the pantry? And on a deeper level, is he just acting like he's happy so that I'll feed him? And let me add that I don't just feed him, I actually cook for him. That's right, cook for him. I don't cook for myself or Jimmy or the kids, yet for this little Shih Tzu, I turn into Mario Batali. Whether it's me he loves or my spice rack is irrelevant. He can use me all he wants because I actually enjoy taking care of him. I guess we both get what we need in the long run.

And on yet one more hand (he has four paws, after all), he's got me just where he wants me, because there is always the implicit threat that he can destroy my house. He can pee and poop everywhere, and there's nothing I can do about it except clean it up. He can go into my closet and chew my best Jimmy Choos or decide that my expensive couch tastes tangy and delicious, and guess what? Nothing I can do. Yeah, I can lock him in the bathroom, but any dog I've ever had has known full well that I'm not going to do that. Luckily, Sumo's never acted out of spite, but I see it in his eyes. He wants me living in fear, I just know it.

Who owns whom? But even being owned is not so bad. I kind of like being owned and manipulated if it means I get all that (what I perceive to be) unconditional love in return.

There's only one really negative aspect to owning dogs, and it's not their fault. They've got a short life span. Not short compared to a fruit fly or a drummer in a punk band, but short compared to a gorilla or one of the Gabor sisters. I think that's why they're so great. All of their time on earth is mushed into twelve or so short years, so they don't have time to waste being assholes and learning and growing. But it does mean that if you've got a dog, you're probably going to have to live through your dog's death. I've been through several, and it's horrible. It's taken me years to get over each and every one of them; yet as painful as each successive death is, I always get another dog.

When Sumo dies, I'll rescue yet another Shih Tzu. I love the breed. They're small, not yippy, and have great temperaments. They were bred to sit on the laps of Chinese emperors, so they're calm, a bit stubborn, haughty, and hypoallergenic. Shih Tzus are the perfect breed for me. If only they knew how to make a great moo shoo.

As a dog lover, I've researched many different breeds, and I've begun to realize that you can tell a lot about a person by what breed of dog they choose to associate with. My research has shown, and this is kind of fascinating, that you can even tell how a man will behave in bed by what breed of dog he has. I'm not kidding. First of all, the fact that a man has a dog in the first place is a good sign because it means that he's capable of taking care of (and hopefully, picking up after) something other than himself. It also indicates that he has a nurturing side. That's the general, but when you begin to look at specific breeds, it's uncanny how accurate this science is as a measure of a man's sexual behavior. Although technically my evidence is more anecdotal than scientific, I can assure you that the results are 100 percent accurate.

Take, for example, men with terriers. They are almost always premature ejaculators. Good news if you're in a hurry, but to be honest, how often are you really that pressed for time? And this isn't supposition, it's fact. Jack Russells are particularly fast and furious dogs, so at all costs avoid dating a guy who has one. Unless, of course, you like that sort of thing, which some women do. Personally, it's not for me. If I'm going to interrupt my busy day for a man, and have to shower before *and* afterwards, it's got to be for a lot more than five minutes of frenzied humping.

Men with Great Danes? Grandiose. It's all about them and their long legs, sleek bodies, and imposing physiques. Lovely to look at but they'll never really *see* you, if you know what I mean. They're Adonises; they know it, they know you know it, and they'll never let you forget it.

Labs? Who doesn't love a Lab? They're sweet, playful, and great with kids. Oh, and they're gentle. A little too gentle. You think everything is fine and dandy, but by the third or fourth date you realize there are follow-through problems. Good for a make-out session, but instant flaccidity may occur at inopportune moments. If you're just into cuddling, this is a good guy for you. If you like something a bit more vigorous, move on.

Beagle? Never, never, ever a beagle. Yeah, I know all about Snoopy and how cute beagles are, but they are as dumb as a box of rocks and virtually untrainable. So what happens? You're in bed with a beagle owner and you say, "Yeah, that's it. Right there. That's the spot. No, no, yes, yes, yes, there, right there," and not five minutes later you have to tell him all over again, and again the next night, and the night after that. Zero retention. Why can't they remember? I don't know. I never have a problem finding it, but a beagle owner might as well be Lewis and Clark seeking the Northwest Passage or Ponce de Leon in search of the fountain of youth.

Speaking of youth, a guy with a basset hound is usually a good bet if you're a little long in the tooth. Their balls, like their ears, may be dragging on the floor, but they'll accept whatever is hanging on you without judgment.

A bit self-conscious about your cellulite? A guy with a shar-pei is for you. They're hard to find, but cheaper than lipo.

There are certain obvious ones:

39

- **Doberman pinscher** Definitely a sadomasochist. Unless you enjoy having a red ball taped in your mouth during sex, avoid, avoid, avoid.

- **Boxer** Oh, so needy. No matter what you do, it is never enough. And while we all like to *feel* needed, actually *being* needed is a huge pain in the ass.

- **Rottweiler** A closet case who likes to play dress-up and has a weird penchant for uniforms. Especially chauffeur's hats.

- **Dalmatian** He'll tell you that his spots are an allergic reaction. Bullshit. He's got herpes. This puppy has spent way too much time at the sniffing post. Remember, when you walk this dog, you're walking every other person who's walked him before.

- **Saint Bernard** Drooler. Nobody likes to sleep in the wet spot.

- **Rhodesian Ridgeback** Mmmmm. Gotta love that ridge!

- **Whippet** The name says it all. Puts the *f* in kinky.

- **Pit bull** Lots of shame issues about past behavior. With extensive therapy, they can sometimes be molded into worthwhile boyfriends, but there's always that chance that he could snap. Some girls find that exciting, but I'm not one of them. Teeth marks never turned me on.

- **German shepherd** Workaholic. Any man who has a pet that is on duty 24/7—helping the blind, sniffing for bombs, caring for the elderly—will have no time for you. On the positive side, he carries a big staff.

- **Husky** Lesbian.

- **Bullmastiff** Big lesbian.

- **Mutt** I have a soft spot for mutts. These guys often come from broken homes, raised by a single parent. The mutt man may be an exotic, sexy, ethnic potpourri, but beware, he also has abandonment issues.

Some breeds are not so obvious and only perceptible to the trained eye. For example, many women are turned off if a man has a Maltese or Shih Tzu, toy poodle, Chihuahua, Pomeranian, papillon, or Chinese crested hairless. Big mistake. Don't be so superficial. Think about it. If a hetero guy is secure enough in his sexuality to carry around a faggy little dog like that, then he must be good in bed. Hold onto this guy and learn how to ignore those nasty little innuendos from so-called friends. The hell with them and their narrow-minded suspicions. Trust me, this one's a keeper.

My own personal favorite is the bloodhound. They're droopy and funny looking, but I like a guy who gets my scent and then pursues me to the ends of the earth. Maybe I'm just insecure, but being with a guy who desires me no matter how strong my odor is seems like a good deal. He's not the kind of guy who's going to get grossed out if your legs aren't shaved or, God forbid, you are menstruating. All he wants to do is get a good whiff and a little sumpin' sumpin', and by God, he's gonna get it. Sounds good to me.

If you're more into the unattainable aloof thing, then look for a man with a cat but never, under any circumstance, a man with more than two of them. Multiple cat owners are smelly and weird, and, chances are, every night before he goes to bed, he has long, heartfelt conversations with the pictures of elderly women he keeps taped to the walls of his closet. Creepy.

So now that I've given you the 411 on men and dogs, go out and rescue one! A dog, not a man. I think the only thing better than having a dog might be being one. In fact, if I were going to be reincarnated, I'd want to come back as a Shih Tzu of a childless older gay couple. Boy, would that be the life!

CHAPTER
4

THE BUSINESS
OF COMEDY,
PART ONE—

I HAD
A DREAM

Susie Essman, age 9

One recent night, I had a great dream. There was some kind of party for me. It wasn't my birthday, but people were bringing gifts. In walked Rose Marie, from *The Dick Van Dyke Show*, with a little black bow in her hair. She gave me a gift. Then Betty White came in and gave me a gift. I was touched. And last but not least, Vivian Vance came in and handed me a gift and said something like, "We are passing on the torch to you as a female sidekick in television comedies." Vivian was in a 1950s shantung shirtwaist and looked great. I was overwhelmed. I took all three gifts and put them in a big red box. That's all I remember. Not exactly the world-changing dream Martin Luther King, Jr. shared with us, but I woke up smiling.

Even though as a kid I was convinced I was an incredibly gifted theatrical prodigy, I never wanted to play Laura Petrie, or Mary Richards, or Lucy Ricardo. It was the roles of Sally Rogers and Sue Ann Nivens and Ethel Mertz that appealed to me. Lucy, as funny as she was, had to go through some kind of manipulative machinations every time she wanted to get Ricky to buy her a new hat. I hated that. Even in elementary school my feminist radar was well honed. I didn't know that's what it was, but while Ricky was at Club Babalu singing, dancing, and laughing, Lucy was home, washing dishes, making beds, and getting her toe stuck in the faucet. Ethel seemed much more in control of her life. Laura Petrie was a stay-at-home mom in New Rochelle, while Sally was in the city writing comedy. True, she didn't have a man, but she did have tons of fun and was doing something creative and interesting. And later on, when I was in high school and college, it was clear to me that Sue Ann, with her tart tongue and lascivious ways, was a much more fun part to portray than Mary.

For as long as I can remember, I wanted to be an actress. As a toddler, I think my first words were, "What's my motivation?" When I was in first grade, we put on a school play. The lead female part was Mrs. Claus (Santa's wife, of course), which I wanted but was given to my best friend, Lisa Kor. At first I thought that I didn't get the part because I was Jewish, but since Lisa was also Jewish, there went my opportunity to be the youngest person to file a claim with the Anti-Defamation League. Although in retrospect, why were we doing a Christmas play in the first place? At least half the class was Jewish! I could have cried discrimination and made a big stink and insisted on singing a solo of "The Dreidel Song" as compensation for damages, but that's not how I wanted to get a part. Instead, I was given some small non-speaking role as a teddy bear. I remember thinking what morons they were—not for mounting a Christmas play for a class full of Jews but because they didn't recognize talent when they saw it. Didn't they know I was the best actress in the class? Somehow, at six years old, I was absolutely positive that I had this ability and thought anyone who didn't see it was an idiot. (To this day, I'm good friends with Lisa Kor and have long since stopped resenting her for taking the part that should have rightly been mine. Someday, perhaps during my first Oscar acceptance speech,

I'll be able to forgive those teachers their ignorance and their anti-Semitism.)

One small part followed another, until one day—one summer, really—as my frustration and bitterness over years and years of not being cast as a lead grew, something happened. I was eight years old and at sleepaway camp. That summer my age group did a production of *The Wizard of Oz* (a camp play if ever there was one!)

Needless to say, I assumed I should play Dorothy. Even though I thought auditioning was a formality, I did it anyway. I sang "Somewhere over the Rainbow" and welled up with tears at just the right moments. My voice was lilting, and I swear, you'd have actually thought I was a farm girl from Kansas. Emerald City, here I come! I was a shoo-in. WRONG! They gave the part to some melodically challenged little blonde who couldn't act her way out of a paper bag.

I got cast as guess whom? Yup, The Wicked Witch of the West. A good part—an important part—but not the lead. Even worse, in Camp Willoway's production of the play, the Wicked Witch had no lines. NONE! When have you ever heard of a mute witch? The witch's entire part, including her melting death scene, was supposed to be done in pantomime. I hate pantomime!

That was it. I had had it. It was clear that I was going to have to take the matter into my own hands. I went to the counselor/director of the play and asked if it was okay if I wrote my own lines. She must have been an "actor's counselor," because she gladly accepted my offer. So I wrote my own death scene. I tried to make it original, without copying or marginalizing Margaret Hamilton's great work, but I did throw in a few "I'm meltings" because I was, in fact, melting. (The camp, which had a wonderful theater group, unfortunately had no air-conditioning.)

The night of the performance, the entire camp was crammed into the rec hall. At the dénouement in the witch's castle, when the little blonde threw the bucket of water on me, I performed the scene I had written. It was a performance for the ages. Every bit of emotion my eight-year-old body could muster was out there on that stage. The rec hall was riveted. It was my moment in the spotlight and I milked it for all it was worth. I was going to show Camp Willoway what real acting was all about. Pantomime my ass.

After I melted all the way to the ground, I was supposed to slip behind the curtain and disappear, but before I could slip away, the audience began to stand and cheer, and I had to rise from the dead and take multiple bows before I trium-phantly walked off the stage. Even the boy playing Toto got up on his hind legs and clapped. Later, during the curtain call, I got more applause than Dorothy. The no-talent little blonde practically had to prostrate herself before me. Finally!

I learned two significant lessons that night: (1) If I was go-ing to get what I wanted, I would have to make it happen my-self, and (2) it was more fun to play the witch than Dorothy. I was hooked and knew, right then and there, that I wanted to be not an actress but a character actress. I was never go-ing to be able to compete with the pretty little blondes of the world, and there were a lot of them out there. Let them fight each other over those boring wimpy ingénue roles. Give me the meaty parts. I wanted to play the witches and the funny girls. And maybe one day, I'd get really lucky and be able to combine the two.

The rest of elementary school was smooth sailing. A string of parts followed. I was fast becoming known as the Rosalind Russell of Mount Vernon, New York. I was riding high, the toast of the town; and then, slam crash boom—a cataclysmic event occurred that destroyed my supreme confidence and the absolute certainty of my own talent. Puberty. Self-consciousness reigned. Boy consciousness ruled.

Remember Sally Rogers? My idol from *The Dick Van Dyke Show*? She was funny as the day was long and equally single. Men were always intimidated by her sense of humor. Her wit might have made them laugh, but it didn't make them hot. In fact, more often than not, it scared them away. Everyone laughed with Sally but no one went home with her. I began to downplay my funniness. If you ask people who knew me in high school if I was funny in those days, those who knew me best, my siblings and my close girlfriends, would say absolutely yes; but others, boys and acquaintances, would say no. I became a closet funny person and only revealed my true self to those I trusted.

I was confused. Being funny was never something I worked at. It was innate. You can't teach timing. It's a rhythm in your body that's either there or not. When I was about five, my parents bought the Mel Brooks/Carl Reiner album, the 2000 *Year Old Man.* I listened to that album constantly. I couldn't possibly have gotten most of the jokes (I was only five), but I knew instinctively that they were funny and I knew why they were funny: the timing. I memorized that album and used to stand up on the kitchen table and perform the whole thing—both parts. My father, who was a good doctor but a lousy joke teller, used to frequently quote lines from the album, but he'd always get it wrong and change the rhythm of the thing. Add a word or two or put something in the wrong order or put emphasis on the wrong syllable, it was like nails on a blackboard; drove me crazy. It was as though I had perfect pitch and he was singing flat.

You can't learn timing and you can't learn point of view or sensibility. You've either got 'em or you don't.

As a kid, I was always performing in one way or another. One year my sister Nora got a portable reel-to-reel tape recorder for Chanukah. I spent hours playing talk show host and guest. When I was ten, my brother Elliot, who was five years older than me, would come home after high school with his friends and they'd smoke pot and then get me to perform for them. I'd stand up on the kitchen counter and pull canned goods out of the cabinets and improvise commercials and do imitations of people we knew and sing "Hip Baby," a Bessie Smith blues parody I wrote. I was their own personal little comedian, the way Pat Henry was for Sinatra. They thought I was hilarious, although in retrospect, maybe they were just stoned. Still, as good as I was doing schtick in the kitchen, it never occurred to me to be a comedian, and certainly not a stand-up comedian. I saw those people on *Ed Sullivan,* and they told jokes. I had no idea how to write jokes. I was just having fun and doing what came naturally. Being myself. Being funny.

But puberty took that away from me as well. Enter hormones, exit humor. Well, not humor really, or timing; just the ability to put it out there, the confidence. I no longer thought I was good enough. Embarrassment crept in. Fear of humiliation. And while my siblings and their oft-stoned friends had always encouraged and enjoyed me, my parents were not quite as pleased with my behavior. "Stop showing off" was a favorite refrain of my father's, and my mother didn't seem to relish my ability to get attention. My sister, Nora, was naturally shy and quiet, and my mother told me in no uncertain terms that I was not to take the spotlight and leave my sister out. This was my mother's issue—not my sister's. My sister has always been my greatest supporter. We were born with two different temperaments and that was fine with us, but there were many times when my mother reminded me to not be "too big" or shine too bright. "Be less" was the message I was getting from everyone everywhere. "Be smaller." "Don't draw attention to yourself." "Be ladylike." "Don't have so many opinions." I was, after all, "just a girl."

That's not to say that I suddenly became a shrinking violet (not my style). I remember high school as fun. I fell in love at fifteen and was pretty wrapped up in that relationship for a number of years, on and off through college. He was two years older than me, and I started hanging out with an older crowd with him. It was the early seventies. I didn't care much about school and quite often didn't even go. I was very political and obsessed with Watergate and into music and photography and books. But the performer in me was lying dormant. I stopped trying out for school plays, not because I didn't want to do then but because I didn't think I was good enough; and as for comedy, well, the boys were supposed to be the funny ones. I didn't compete.

When it came time to go to college, I really had no interest. I only applied to one school—State University of New York at Purchase. It was a brand-new state school and not far from home (I've always had agoraphobic tendencies). It was known primarily as an arts school and had a great theater department. But the thought of applying to the theater department was way too scary to even think about. I had to audition for that. I didn't want to put myself through the humiliation of that process. I figured I could register as a liberal arts major and simply take some theater classes.

I applied and got in and went because, as I said, it was the only school I applied to. Once there, I quickly found out that you couldn't dabble in theater. Purchase was a conservatory, where you were either a theater major or not. And boy, was I intimidated by those theater majors. They were all these flamboyant theatrical types. Pretentious guys in suits carrying attaché cases, wearing white silk scarves around their necks. Or thin wispy guys who constantly and, for no apparent reason, burst into song. The girls were all overly dramatic and seemed very mature and sophisticated. They all behaved as though they had just stepped off the set of *All About Eve*.

In my second semester I took a class called "acting for non-majors." Even the name was condescending. It was as ridiculous as "surgery for non-doctors." In the first class we had to do all these exercises like go and stand in the corner and pretend you're a pear for half an hour. And then we had to walk around the room with our eyes shut and touch each other and then open our eyes and tell the person we were touching what we were thinking. It was a load of shit. I quit after that first class and gave up any thoughts of following my dream for a few years.

One night, toward the end of my senior year, I was watching TV with a bunch of friends in lieu of studying, which I often did. We were watching *The Carol Burnett Show* and my friend Nancy said, "Susie, you can do that. That's what you should be doing." And it struck me, she was right. How Nancy Magline knew what my parents and advisors didn't, I have no idea, I just know that I heard what she said and it changed my life. At heart I was a comedic actress, and that's what I was meant to be doing. I had known that at six years old, yet no one had ever said it to me before. On the contrary, I had heard just the opposite. Everyone had thought I was crazy when I'd told them what my heart's desire was. As a matter of fact, my boyfriend at that time, who was in law school, told me that wanting to be an actress was the most ridiculous thing he'd ever heard. I can only imagine what he would've said if I'd told him I wanted to be a cannibal tap dancer. But Nancy's suggestion was so matter-of-fact that in that moment, she made me realize something I already knew but hadn't been able to see because I'd been filled with misinformation. The day after I graduated college with a degree in urban studies, I began taking acting classes in Manhattan.

My problems were not immediately solved. I wasn't getting the creative charge from the acting classes that I thought I'd get. Truth be told, I found it kind of boring. I was twenty-two then. I wouldn't get on stage and attempt stand-up until I was twenty-eight. Six years of floundering, trying to figure out what I was supposed to be doing with my life.

It was not a particularly happy six years. I was lost, living in Manhattan, and waitressing, occasionally taking acting classes and occasionally appearing in small showcases. While that kind of life seems romantic in movies and television, in reality it's not. It's a struggle, financially, physically, and emotionally. The only real structure I had in my life was my waitress job, and in order to bear that, I entertained myself and my fellow workers by imitating all the customers. I built up a whole slew of regular characters I did. I was ten again, standing on the kitchen table, performing for my brother's stoned friends.

My friends and coworkers encouraged me to do something with my funniness. But what? I was too paralyzed with fear to do anything. To make matters worse, in 1980, when I was twenty-five, I got into a bad relationship. A really bad one, an all-consuming, deeply enmeshed, bad relationship that lasted for four years on and off. Like me, he was also a wannabe actor and also funny but we were ill-suited for one another and brought out each other's worst aspects. The never-ending drama and emotional rollercoaster ride was the perfect distraction. As a couple our highs were high and our lows were low. We were inseparable and fought frequently. We were *that* couple. None of our friends liked being with us when we were together. We were addicted to one another and created our own little isolated world. For a few years, it felt womblike and safe, until it almost killed me.

Looking back, I don't know what I was thinking. How could I have been so stupid and careless? Inevitably everything crashed. By 1983, I was beginning to fall apart. I felt bad about myself all the time. Things were getting desperate. I frequently had suicidal thoughts. That was new but felt comforting to know that I had the option. Not that I wanted to die, but I wanted the pain to go away and it was also the only way I thought I'd ever be able to extricate myself from the relationship I was in. I felt trapped. I couldn't leave him. How could I possibly survive without him? Every morning I woke up and it was still there, that horrible feeling of despair so deep that I couldn't see my way through it. I found a good therapist. I asked her what that feeling was. "Self loathing" she told me. I started seeing her twice a week.

As unhappy as I was, there were still remnants of that little girl who knew she had talent, who knew that they were all a bunch of morons for not seeing it. It was hard to hold onto that; especially since my boyfriend was not only bad for me but also competitive. The first time he and my father met, they had a discussion in front of me, as though I wasn't even in the room, about how bad my acting was in a play they had both seen me perform in. Is it any wonder that I didn't get onstage in any form again for three years?

Most artists know when they have real talent. The voice may be faint and it may lay dormant and buried for years, insecurity may feel all-encompassing, but there's a place deep inside that knows how good we are. I had to get back to that place, to the time when I got more applause than Dorothy, to the time before I was shut down and shut up by life and environment and circumstance. I had to do something to shake things up—to change. I was desperate.

In April 1983, I registered for two classes. One was an improv class at the YMCA, and the other was a stand-up class at Manhattan Punchline. I had no intention of pursuing either, but I needed to do something. I was barely functional at this point. I told myself, *Just move forward. Something's gotta give. It can't get much worse.* At about the same time, my boyfriend broke up with me, kind of. We'd been down this road before, but this time, I felt a little better about it. I knew we'd get back together, we always did; but I wanted a break from him and he provided me with it. I couldn't have moved forward with his judgmental eyes always on me. Without sounding overly dramatic, I felt like I was fighting for my life.

The improv class was fun. We did a series of in-class exercises in which we had to be quick and in the moment. I was good at it. I was at a point where I needed to be good at something, and that gave me a boost of confidence. The stand-up class was a whole other animal. We had actual assignments. The first class, the teacher gave us subjects to write about—family, politics, whatever—and we had to bring it in the following week and perform it as a monologue. This was too much for me—actually writing down what I thought was funny. Improvising in the moment was one thing, but actually committing to saying "I think this is funny" on paper was more than I could bear.

I cut the next class because I was afraid to write anything. It was physically painful for me to even try. But then the following week I forced myself to go back, and I improvised something with one of the other comedians. I did characters and he interviewed me and it worked. There was a glimmer of something. I saw that there was a possibility that I could do this. Some of the people in the class had been going up on stage at open mic nights around the city. Those were nights when anyone could show up, and I mean *anyone,* and get onstage. Most of these places weren't even full-time comedy clubs—they were bars or restaurants or cabarets that did comedy one night a week. They were all over the city, and they gave performers a chance to make people laugh.

One open-mic night was at a club called Mostly Magic, downtown in the Village, and on Tuesday, July 19, 1983, when I was twenty-eight years old, I went to Mostly Magic on Carmine Street to pick a number and get onstage in front of a room full of strangers. I had put together five minutes in which I played four different characters: a young Latina girl who was the president of the Menudo fan club, a waspy Connecticut woman, a Jewish mother type, and a jappy Long Island girl. I went from one character to another and never spoke in my own voice. I had a little red plastic attaché case, and I had a few props, a hat or something that I put on to indicate a change. I don't remember the exact material, but I remember the anxiety. As I write this, twenty-six years later, I can still feel the anxiety. I have never been so scared in my life. I remember sitting on the floor of my apartment before I left the house and rocking back and forth endlessly, like I was either davening or on Darvon. I felt sick to my stomach. I felt like I was going to die.

I couldn't back out, because all my friends were going to

be at Mostly Magic to support me. What had I been thinking? Was it not enough drama to go onstage in front of total strangers? Had I really needed to invite friends to witness my public humiliation? The answer was yes. I needed them. I couldn't have done it without them, and while I made lousy choices in boyfriends, I had a gift for friendship, and it always served me well.

By the time I got to the club I was literally shaking. Suddenly, the emcee called my name and it was my turn to hit the stage. I went up with my little red case and did the entire five minutes I'd planned in about a minute and a half. I was racing, but I got laughs. Then it was over. I was done.

Afterward, something unexpected happened. These two older guys, about fortyish (back then they were older) came over to me and introduced themselves. They were Paul Herzich and Burt Leavitt. They told me they were opening up a comedy club in a couple of months and they wanted me to come work at their club. I gave them my number and never expected to hear from them.

I honestly had no plans to get onstage again anytime soon, because despite my quasi-successful first attempt at comedy, the depression deepened. Get onstage? Unless that stage was next to my bed, I didn't see that happening. I could barely leave the house. I tried to socialize with friends, but since I cried *all the time,* and I mean all the time, I wasn't much fun to be with. My boyfriend was no longer in the picture and was seeing someone else. (Don't worry, he'd resurface once again a few months later. He was the gift that kept on giving.)

If you've never experienced true depression, I'm sure it's

hard to fathom. It's just as difficult to describe. I'm not talking about sadness or just being in a bad mood. I'm talking a deep, dark place where there is no light. I didn't see any end in sight. When you're in it, that awful abyss, you can't imagine that you'll ever feel better again and you don't trust that the darkness will ever lift. Earlier, in the beginning of July 1983, right before I got on stage at Mostly Magic, suicidal thoughts were increasing. At the suggestion of my therapist, I started psychoanalysis in an attempt to understand why I was so unhappy. I went to her office four days a week, laid on the couch and free-associated. (This was a time before Prozac became one of America's four basic food groups. If I was ever going to get better, I was going to have to do the work slowly and painfully. No shortcuts.)

I never did figure out "the answer." I don't think there was one. Would I have simply outgrown the depression without all the therapy? Maybe, but I wasn't willing to take that chance. There's always plenty of blame to go around. My mother, my father, sexism, boyfriends, hormones, who knows? Everything and nothing. Ultimately, the blame was meaningless because the only person who had any control over my feelings was me. So I spent nine years on the couch and asked endless questions that I knew there were no answers to. It was one of the best things I've ever done. It saved my life.

The other lifesaver was stand-up. It was unexpected. I had absolutely no plan at all, and then fate intervened.

One day, in mid-September 1983, a long two months since my comedy debut at Mostly Magic, I got a call from Burt Leavitt. I had forgotten about those guys. I was too busy wallowing in my own pain and misery. Besides which, stand-up wasn't something I was going to pursue. Herzich and Leavitt had opened the club. It was in the Village on University Place, and it was called Comedy U. Burt wanted to know if I would come down the following Sunday and do ten minutes onstage. I said I'd be there. I have no idea why I said I'd be there. I didn't have ten minutes of material, and I was clinically depressed. What was I going to do? Stand up onstage and sob for ten minutes? I was a psychological mess! Asking me to do ten minutes of stand-up was like asking Sylvia Plath to tell some knock-knock jokes. Besides, I wasn't even a comedian, but some survival instinct in me said yes.

In retrospect, if I hadn't been in such dire straits, I probably never would have done it. I needed to save myself, and this seemed like as good a bet as any. If I had had another career, or even if there had been something else I liked to do, I wouldn't have put myself through the agony of getting onstage in front of strangers and having them expect me to make them laugh. It was so hard. It is still hard, but it's even more so in the beginning, when you have no experience and technique and are filled with self-doubt. It was pure agony. But nothing could have been as painful as where I had already been. So I painstakingly wrote ten minutes of material for my characters and went down there and did it.

It went okay. Not bad, not good. But these guys just seemed to like me, and they invited me back for their Thursday "women in comedy night." I showed up on Thursday, and there were all these female comedians who all knew each other and all seemed so cool, and I felt so intimidated. It was the theater majors all over again. I didn't belong. I was an outsider. I wasn't good enough. They all knew something that I didn't. I went on late in the evening after sitting there watching these more experienced and savvy women, one after another. Finally, when it was my turn, I went on and the audience laughed at everything I said.

It was my third time onstage, and I had a killer set. I'd never felt exhilaration like that before. It was incredible. It was so powerful.

I was flying high that night, but the next day, I felt even worse than I had before. I didn't think it was possible to go even further into the abyss, but here it was. My success had pushed me over the brink. I don't know why, but to stand up there onstage all by myself and speak and be acknowledged and recognized seemed like I had committed the worst crime possible. I wasn't allowed to get all that attention. I wanted to die. I wanted relief from the pain. I showed up crying at my then ex-boyfriend's (yeah, same one) apartment, and he was cold to me, rejecting. That night, I took every pill in my medicine cabinet from aspirin to Valium to Tums and laid down on my sofa, hoping to die. Somehow, and I don't know how long it took, I got up and called my best friend Jane and then my father. I told him what I had done. He instructed me to stick my fingers down my throat and try to vomit. I did, and the rest is a blur.

A few days later, I was staying at my parents' house, recuperating and still somewhat out of it, when Burt called and told me they wanted to give me a paid weekend spot. I had been told by other comics that I shouldn't expect a paid spot for at least two years. These guys were going to make me a comedian whether I wanted it or not. I knew that I had to get up there again. I had tasted the fruit. Besides, I was so sick of my unhappiness, and there was no place else to go. I had decided to live, so if I was going to stick around, I might as well do something with my life. There was something about actually having acted on my suicidal thoughts that banished them. Death no longer felt like an option. No matter how scared I was or how poorly I did onstage, nothing could ever feel as bad as I had when I'd wanted to die. I had nothing to lose and everything to gain.

I did the paid weekend spot. I went onstage, got my laughs, and when I came off, Burt and Paul handed me a twenty-dollar bill. I still have it. I actually made money making people laugh. I couldn't believe it. They kept giving me spots and I kept working on my act. I worked exclusively at Comedy U for the first six months of my comedy career. I was lucky. I had a safe place where I could figure out who I was and what I wanted to be. I remember the moment about three months into it, when I realized my friend Nancy was right. I could do this and I should do this. I was doing the exact thing that I was supposed to be doing. I had found my calling.

I always knew that eventually I would have to expand and leave the comfort of the Comedy U womb. If I'd had to go immediately into the highly competitive environment of the big uptown showcase clubs, however, I don't know that I could have done it. I was too fragile.

The depression slowly and steadily abated, and I regained focus and purpose and got lots of positive reinforcement. I was having fun and I wasn't miserable anymore. What a relief it was when that feeling was no longer there. I remember waking up one morning, about a month after the failed suicide attempt, and the feeling of despair that had been my constant companion was gone. A few months later the boyfriend returned, but by then I was a different person. I was a working comedian. We tried to make it work one more time, and when it finally ended for good, I felt as though a disease had left my body. I'd almost committed suicide. I'd almost given in to it. But instead I survived and was resurrected as a comedian, of all things. It's ironic that stand-up saved my life, because over the past twenty-five years, there have been times when performing has been so arduous that I've felt like it was going to kill me. Pick your poison.

As I reflect back on the career path I took, I realize that I was in denial about the difficulty of what I was embarking on. If I'd known how hard it was going to be, would I have done it anyway? I think I would have, yes. I hadn't had a choice. I'd *had* to do it.

Little did I know, I was trading in my depression for a lifetime of anxiety.

CHAPTER
5

WEATHER
PORN

There's no easy way to say this, but my husband is into three-ways. Every night when we dim the lights and crawl into bed, there's always someone else with us, and it's always the same person— no, not Sumo, my Shih Tzu, but Jim Cantore. That's right, Jim Cantore, crack meteorologist and storm chaser extraordinaire; the man who puts the ayayay in isobar, the man who is the face of the Weather Channel. *That* Jim Cantore. He's the last person my husband sees at night and the first person he looks at in the morning, and I'm pretty sure that between sunset and sunrise, he dreams about him too. My husband is in love, I just know it. A woman knows these things about her man. And even though it's not a physical relationship, just an emotional one, isn't that just as dangerous? Maybe even more so? You can't shower away feelings. And yet, I'm not nearly as resentful as I might be; in fact, I understand how Jimmy feels. I like Jim Cantore too.

Why wouldn't I? Why wouldn't anyone? If there's a tornado, Cantore is there. If there's a hurricane, he's in the eye of it. Floods, droughts, blizzards, monsoons . . . He's Johnny on the spot. And not only is he there but he's there with fervor, thrilled to be in harm's way. I've never seen anyone get this worked up over weather conditions . . . except, of course, my husband.

Having Jim Cantore in all his weather-beaten manglory on

TV at the foot of the bed is not as bad as it sounds, particularly when you look at the other broadcast options available. Think about it. There are nine hundred cable channels, each with their own set of stars and personalities. Jimmy could have his choice of any one of them for our nightly ménage à trois.

For example, he could've fallen for Nancy Grace, Court TV's resident virago. Can you imagine what a horror that would be? Forget the relentless scolding and hectoring; every time she'd reach orgasm, she'd scream out the name of some battered woman or kidnapped child desperate for justice! Now that's a real turn-on!

Or he could have developed the hots for one of those obnoxious TV pitchmen who are always yelling at the top of his lungs about some mop or Chamois cloth or cutting tool that can core an apple, chop an onion, or saw through a car to rescue a trapped kitten. Having one of them scream sweet nothings in my ear every night would cause chafing for sure.

I generally don't like to watch the news before I go to sleep. Too disturbing. But there was one CNN correspondent that I used to have the hots for and enjoyed watching, that is until he did something drastic to his appearance. I don't want to mention any names, but about a year ago this White House correspondent had some major glistening veneers put on his teeth and now he can't close his mouth or pronounce *P*'s, *B*'s or *M*'s. He says things like "refuflican" and "devocrat." His new smile frightens me. I don't think I want him near my fussy.

And no, I'm not referring to Wolf Blitzer. He would be fine. Believe it or not, I've always had a fantasy about sleeping with him, and not because I find him so attractive. He's alright I guess; it's just that I always thought it would be cool to be eaten by a wolf.

So you see, Jim Cantore is not such a bad choice after all. I think Jimmy's obsession with him may be based on some kind of identity confusion issues. Both of them are named Jim, and they both have shaved heads, and they're both hunky and cute and sexy, and they both get their kicks from fluctuations of the barometric pressure. How weird is that? What are the odds?

My Jim, or Jimmy as I call him, is a climatophobe; he has the Weather Channel on whenever he's home, sort of like background music, the way right-wing nut jobs always have talk radio playing somewhere in the house. I am not exaggerating. He even DVRs "Storm Stories," and whenever they have a tornado special, well, he's positively orgasmic. He revels in this stuff. I call this fascination "weather porn." It's addictive, and once you start watching it, you just can't turn away. Ordinary sunny, balmy days just don't cut it anymore. And partly cloudy with scattered showers seems outright insipid. I understand it. Is there anything more arousing than the powerful visual of a hurricane or a typhoon? The destruction and devastation are mesmerizing. Collapsed houses, burning forests, melting mountains, flooded streets, frozen plains . . . And though the weather may always be changing, the one constant is that Jim Cantore is out there, fearless and selfless, braving the elements. He's out there, in the rain and snow, wind and sleet, sacrificing for all of us, putting his life on the line every day, just so we know whether to wear a marvelous little outfit from Ann Taylor or to opt for a London

Fog parka and rubbers. He's like Jesus, getting soaked for our sins.

Don't get me wrong, I'm not weather bashing—I watch the Weather Channel too. It's a wonderful network, where every eight minutes you can get your local forecast. That's really all I care about. Jimmy cares about the weather all over the world. He's a much better person than I am. He's even philosophical about it. He believes, and rightly so, that weather is the great equalizer that proves how little control we have. It's very humbling. Yeah, we've got all this technology and intelligence and information, but weather is the big "fuck you" to us all. The real boss is mother nature herself. It's nice to be with a man who believes in ultimate female power.

Sometimes Jimmy and I like to watch the channel together. In fact, we particularly enjoy cuddling during flood season. I think that one of the keys to the success of our relationship is that for the most part we like to watch the same things on TV. We both like to watch sports and anything having to do with ancient civilizations and animals and nature and evolution and anthropology and science and old movies.

But like most couples, we don't agree on everything. There are shows he likes and I don't, and vice versa. I love *Mad Men* on AMC. Jimmy hates when I watch that show because all of the men are cheating on their wives, every single one of them, and invariably, when I watch it, I accuse him of cheating on me. I know, it's totally irrational and it's based on nothing, but I'm absolutely sure I'm right. If the guys on *Mad Men* are cheating and they're all married, ergo my husband must be doing it too. Jimmy likes shows like *Ax Men* and *How It's*

Made, Dirty Jobs and *Deadliest Catch,* those kinds of techno/mechanical/fishing-is-somehow-involved boy shows. I'm not interested. Too messy.

LUCKILY, THERE'S usually enough common ground to get us through the night—not to mention more than one television in the house if a conflict does arise. But when it's time to go to bed and I turn the lights off and close my eyes, my husband turns to the Weather Channel like clockwork for one last glimpse of his hero, Jim Cantore, before he drifts off to dreamland. How can I compete with a man in a windbreaker, tethered to a palm tree, in driving rain and 140-mile-an-hour wind gusts? I can't and I won't even try. All I can do is embrace Jimmy's obsession with Jim Cantore and find solace in the fact that it could be worse—he could be in love with Sam Champion.

CHAPTER
6

THE "PAUSE"

I 'm perimenopausal, and I know that I am because I have the symptoms and I know I have the symptoms because I spend 80 percent of my free time checking out the myriad medical sites online. I spend the other 20 percent looking for lumps.

I feel so blessed to live in an age where medical information is available on the internet. Internet info is a hypochondriac's wet dream and a doctor's worst nightmare. I spend a lot of time on these websites checking symptoms for illnesses and conditions I'm certain I have. So far, this month alone, I've had Lyme disease, hysterical blindness, and an enlarged prostate. Whenever someone I know, or someone I know knows someone who has an illness—minor, major, or terminal—I immediately assume I have it too and plan accordingly. Much to my delight and chagrin, almost all of the commercials on TV these days are for some kind of pharmaceutical treatment for diseases I've never heard of but am sure I've contracted. One after another, fifteen-, thirty-, and sixty-second spots for pills and ointments that must be taken at your own risk. I know I'm not alone in this. Otherwise there wouldn't be so many goddamn commercials for this stuff. I've even thought of starting a symptoms checkers support group. I'll call it Dead by Tuesday Anonymous.

The beauty of the internet is that there are so many choices. There's WebMD, MayoClinic.com., MedicineLine

.com, Medicine.net . . . Plus hundreds of specialty sites, too numerous to mention. Let's say I go on WebMD to check a symptom of a disease that I suspect I have, and they inform me that I'm in good health and have nothing to worry about. Needless to say, that prognosis doesn't sit well with me, so I can simply dismiss it and check out the other sites until I find one with an outcome that pleases me, one, that if not fatal, will certainly be very dramatic. The sheer volume of medical websites gives me hope that somewhere, somehow, I can find a site that lists my symptoms and will reinforce my belief that I have something that I most probably don't have a chance in hell of having. A lot of symptoms are universal. So many diseases have symptoms I can easily have. Fatigue. Who's not fatigued? Lethargy? Isn't she the twin sister of lazy? Or bloating? I'm bloated twenty-nine out of thirty-one days of the month! And you can fake yourself out on some symptoms and convince yourself that you have them even when you don't. Dizziness, for example. Dizzy is my middle name. I can easily convince myself that I felt dizzy because I lifted my head up too quickly the other day.

I don't mean to trivialize the pain and suffering of people who are really sick, and it's not that I really want to be sick, but the hypochondria is something that is out of my control. Illness is frightening. If I gain weight I'm convinced it's because I have a tumor growing inside of me that weighs a few pounds. If I lose weight, it's because the tumor is causing a diminished appetite. I can't win. To ease my fears I tell myself that if I'm vigilant about my health, then I'll remain healthy. But there is anecdotal evidence everywhere

I turn that proves that this approach doesn't necessarily work.

Honestly, I'm not that bad, comparatively speaking. I've got a few friends that are pathological hypochondriacs. They make me seem like the bastion of mental health. Their hypochondria colors every moment of their lives, whereas mine simply informs it. You can see the movement behind their eyes the moment someone sneezes in their presence. By the time the sneezer says, "Excuse me," they've already been on the phone with the Centers for Disease Control, three immediate family members, and the head obituary writer for the *New York Times*. The gripping fear makes them incapable of really being a friend, because when you tell them about something wrong with you, all they're really thinking about is whether or not it's going to happen to them. They ask you about your symptoms as though they're being empathetic, but their motives are so transparent.

We all play these games. You hear that a friend has lung cancer and know that they're a smoker. That's an easy one because the cause and effect are so clear. But then another friend has lung cancer and they're not a smoker. Now we're into different territory. Is there a family history? Were they exposed to asbestos? Secondhand smoke? Do they live near a power plant? Did they ever spend a summer with Erin Brockovich? And when there doesn't appear to be any reason for them to have gotten lung cancer, when it's random and arbitrary, then that is proof positive that I, and my severely hypochondriacal friends, must have cancer too.

I grew up in a household that loved disease. Not like, loved.

Sound weird? My father was a doctor and made a living off it, and my mother, according to her self-diagnosis, has been dying since 1963. My father always had medical paraphernalia around the house, syringes and tubes of blood in the refrigerator, and promotional items from drug companies in drawers and cabinets. I remember the pad next to the phone for writing down messages was in the shape of a colon. I'm not kidding. Disease was discussed at the dinner table with regularity. Between the soup and salad we usually had botulism, stroke, and retinitis pigmentosa. Someone in the family or extended family always had something.

For as long as I could remember, each of my parents would pull me aside, individually, to tell me that the other one was deathly ill and dying and then they'd go for a million tests, which they loved, and then there'd be nothing wrong. It was kind of a wish and a fear all rolled up in one.

For example, my mother would pull me aside and say, "I think Daddy has a brain tumor." And then he'd have tests tests tests and there would be nothing wrong. Or my father would say to me, "I think your mother has rickets," and then she'd have tests tests tests and there'd be nothing wrong. It was nutty. Maybe they needed the distraction from the realities of life, I don't know. My father did ultimately get cancer for real and died in 2001, but my mother is still frequently telling me that she's about to die. She's eighty-three, and while she's not in perfect health, she's nowhere near death. She's got lots of aches and pains and trouble with her eyes and ears, but none of her maladies are life threatening. Still, she told me just a few weeks ago that she'll be dead within a few months.

"Really? What from?" I asked.

"Oh, lots of things."

"Name one."

"Well, I've got a heart murmur."

"I've never heard of anyone dying of a heart murmur. And besides, you've had it for years."

"Well, I could drop dead of an aneurism."

"Yeah, well, so could I!"

So you see, I come by my own issues honestly. I get my mammograms and sonograms and pap smears and blood workups and even the dreaded colonoscopy on a regular basis, and I have the dermatologist check my moles and everything is just finefinefine and then I read about some flesh-eating supervirus and I'm instantly convinced that I contracted it on my way home from my checkup. How the hell am I supposed to protect myself from that kind of deadly scourge? By eating more broccoli? You have no idea how much broccoli I already eat, and carrots and beets and even kale, and I don't think a trans fat or anything with corn syrup has crossed these lips in a very long time. I wash my hands frequently, not sick OCD-ishy frequently, although some non-vigilant types may think so, but I can't deny that antibacterial hand lotion and I have become the best of friends.

Allow me to offer you a little hint about antibacterial lotions and gels. To me, they're one of the greatest inventions of all time, right alongside fire, the wheel, and ribbed condoms. Now I know there are naysayers out there who claim that they do nothing, and some say they actually foster bacterial growth. Bullshit. I don't believe a word of it, and I don't care to see the evidence. I choose to believe that these products work and that they're effective and protecting me. A placebo effect perhaps, but whatever gets you through the night.

There are germs everywhere. Go to the ATM and use that touch screen and the chances are that the guy who used it before you had the flu virus all over his fingers. What are the odds that not one person who touched those buttons before you was a nose-picker? You'd better get that gel out, because a sink with soap and hot water is not part of the operation over there.

Hand shaking is also a lightning rod for the spread of germs. People make you out to be crazy or antisocial if you don't want to press the flesh, but I think it's simply self-preservation. Do you know how much crap is spread by hand-to-hand contact? Donald Trump and Howie Mandel do. They don't shake hands with anybody—in fact their hands are probably in pristine condition, clean enough to perform major surgery. On *Deal Or No Deal,* not only does Howie not shake the players' hands, he doesn't even touch those freaking briefcases. A number of years ago, when Donald Trump was running for president, a big deal was made over the fact that he wouldn't shake hands. To me, that's the smartest thing he could possibly have done. I'd vote for him on that issue alone. I roasted Donald Trump at a Friars Roast a couple of years after he ran for office and said, "Everybody thinks that Donald doesn't shake hands because he's a germaphobe, but the truth is, he jerks off so much that he considers anything else cheating." Okay, that was a joke at a roast—and a good one, I might add—but in reality I admire his convictions about hand shaking. I'm too chicken shit and afraid of offending to make that rule, although I should follow his lead. Sometimes when I do a meet and greet after a show and have to shake literally hundreds of people's hands I feign illness and tell them that I have a cold or getting over the flu so I don't want to shake, as though I'm actually protecting them from my germs. My altruism is never-ending.

One of my greatest bacterial challenges is the fact that I travel a lot, which exposes one to all sorts of germs from all over the world. I mostly travel for work, not adventure, which means I'm usually in the comfort of the Pacific Palisades, not on a deserted island in the Pacific Ocean. But even when I'm on vacation, I'm not particularly adventurous. I have no interest in climbing Mount Everest or bungee jumping or sky diving or any activity where I can suffer bodily harm, like breaking my neck, or losing a limb, or tanning unevenly. I take enough risks onstage and onscreen that any further adrenaline rush is totally unnecessary. Do you know how high I feel every time I yell at Larry David? What more can I ask for? Why test the fates? Hiking through the woods exposes you to all kinds of bug bites and poison ivy. The beach is nice, but only under an umbrella, where you're protected from those evil UVA and UVB rays.

For me, a vacation involves great shopping and great restaurants and beauty and a bit of luxury. Not over-the-top luxury— I don't need a diminutive personal manservant to fetch me things and pumice my feet, but I don't think indoor plumbing, air-conditioning, and room service are unreasonable requests. And speaking of indoor plumbing, the thought of camping is horrific. No interest whatsoever. If God wanted us to be camping, she wouldn't have invented The Ritz-Carlton. And even though I'm enormously fascinated by other cultures, if it's a big schlep to get there or I have to be careful about drinking the water or eating the food, or if the visit requires shots beforehand, I'd rather watch the Travel Channel or *Nat Geo* or Robin Leach. My nephew and his wife and daughter live in Australia. I'd love to visit them, but the thought of sitting in a stuffy plane for twenty-two straight hours causes me such fits of anxiety that I don't know if it will ever happen. People tell me that they're dying to go to China, India, Vietnam, Africa. I say, "Enjoy yourself and send me a postcard. I'll be in Miami relaxing, shopping, and eating."

I'm not a big fan of flying. It's not that I'm afraid to fly, it's just that I hate it. I hate the packing and the airport and the germs and the confinement and the germs and the lack of control and, oh, by the way, have I mentioned the germs? Allow me once again to put on my "Susie, the Good" hat and give you some pointers on what to do when you do have to fly somewhere. First of all, always wear socks. Even in the summer. The grossest thing in the world (other than European men wearing brown socks with sandals) is to see someone going through security in flip-flops. They take their shoes off to go through and they're walking barefoot on that floor that thousands of people have walked on before them with all sorts of crap on their shoes. It's disgusting. No different than the horror I feel when I see someone walking barefoot through the streets of New York City. I fear for their life. And I read that the floor at the airport is loaded with staph infection. As is everywhere else. Being barefoot on the plane is even more disgusting, because now, in addition to the normal dirt, schmutz, and dog shit they have on their shoes, they've added to the mix whatever crap they picked up in the airport itself.

Next, sanitize! After I go through the security, I hand sanitize and moisturize like crazy. Always bring moisturizing lotion with you, because the sanitizer, thankfully, is pure alcohol and dries out your hands, so you need to moisturize afterwards. Remember, when you're in an airport, there are people who are passing through from every corner of the globe. They're coming from places with microorganisms and bacteria that you, or anyone in your entire gene pool, have never been exposed to. You have no immunities to this stuff! Try at all costs to avoid the airport bathrooms, unless of course you're a Republican senator from Idaho, in which case, by all means, set up shop. For the rest of you, only use them if you absolutely have to, and remember, don't assume other people are clean. They're not.

Once *on* the plane, get out your wipes and become your own cleaning lady. I use just plain antibacterial ones. My manager uses the alcohol wipes that are wrapped in foil that diabetics use before they inject themselves, which he proudly tells me are three dollars for a pack of five hundred. My friend Robyn Todd travels with a big tub of Clorox wipes. She also turned me on to the benefits of filling your nostrils with Polysporin ointment when you're on the plane. Yeah it's gross and looks like your nose is dripping goo, but at least when you breathe in all that bad air, it's being filtered through an antibiotic barrier. See, I'm not the only crazy one out there. Robyn and I are single-handedly putting the Walgreens' kids through college! Wipe down everything you can reach: seat, tray, table, headphones, the guy sitting next to you . . . Same thing in the bathroom. Wipe, wipe, wipe. Seats, counters, mirrors—if you can wipe down the actual paper towels, do that too. You think they clean those planes between flights? They don't. You have no idea who was lying on that pillow with God knows what kind of head lice or scabies before you.

So, you've arrived at your destination with no new diseases or infections that you know of, and are ready to check into your hotel. Before you even say hello to the concierge, once again, wipe, wipe, wipe. Hotels, even the five-star variety, are a hotbed of germs and bacteria. In five-star hotels you'll get five-star bacteria. Every doorknob, every light switch, the phone, the toilet handle, needs your sanitizing attention. You think the maid is cleaning the toilet handle? NO! And most important of all, clean the remote control. Who knows what movies some businessman from Cincinnati was watching before you got there . . . which leads me to the bedspread, which may reflect the aftermath of the movie he was watching. Eeeeeewwwwww. Hotels wash the sheets and pillowcases, but they don't wash bedspreads or pillow shams between guests, and you have no idea who the prior guests were—not that it matters; just assume they're all pigs. The bedspread is the most disgusting thing in the room, so take it off immediately, throw it in the corner, and go boil your hands. Or better yet, use a hand towel to lift it off the bed so you don't even have to touch the damn thing and ask housekeeping to get rid of it and never bring it back. This goes for duvet covers, blankets, comforters, or anything else that sits on top of the top sheet. Ahh, the top sheet, one of nature's little miracles. Make sure you fold it all the way over the duvet, like a sausage casing, so that no potentially unclean thing is touching any part of your body! Also, bring slippers or flip-flops (the ones you shouldn't wear in the airport) so you don't have to walk on the carpet. Athlete's foot or fungus or crap that dropped off of another person's body could be lurking in those fibers. Similarly, this is why you shouldn't sit naked on the big fluffy overstuffed chair. And speaking of the overstuffed chair, there's a worldwide epidemic of bedbugs in even the swankiest of hotels. Check for brown dried blood spots on the sheets. And don't ever put your suitcase or clothing on the bed or any other piece of upholstered furniture.

The suitcases are a hygiene issue themselves. It's always amazing to me that people will come back from a trip and take their suitcase, which has been in the cargo section of the plane, and put it on their bed to unpack. That thing is filthy! I wipe down my suitcase in my hallway before I even allow it in my house. My sister Nina has a spray bottle with bleach and water in it and sprays the luggage before she allows it in the apartment. Maybe it runs in the family, because my sister Nora is a vigilant germ freak as well, but the truth is, I do think all of these things make a difference. When I walk into a hotel room and take out my wipes, it takes me under a minute to wipe the room down to my satisfaction. Why not play it safe? Sixty seconds of diligent cleaning is well worth gaining sixty years of your life.

Sadly, I'm just one woman, and I can only do what I can do.

The reality is, I can wipe surfaces till my heart's content and there are *still* a million and one other things out there that can wreck havoc on my body. Things like antibiotic-resistant staph infection and spider bites and auto emissions and tainted food and, as I said, I'm perimenopausal.

What exactly is perimenopause? It's the period of time before menopause. They have a name for it now so now it's a condition, when in the past it was just life. Actually, when women say that they're going through menopause, they're really going through perimenopause. Menopause itself lasts for just one day, the day after a woman has not menstruated for one whole year. Then you're officially in menopause. And then it's just life again. There's no "pause" involved. The perimenopause can start at any time and can last for years. And there's really no "pause" involved in that either. It can start as early as thirty-five, but most women begin in their early forties, and it lasts all the way up until that one day when you're finally in menopause. A lot of the symptoms for the perimenopause are the same as for the menopause. For some women the symptoms abate after menopause, but for many, they don't. They go on and on and on. So again, where the hell is the "pause"? I have a friend who went through menopause thirteen years ago and is still suffering from frequent hot flashes.

There is so much to look forward to. I of course went online to check the perimenopause and the menopause symptoms to see what I do and do not have. Interestingly, there were almost no variations of symptoms from website to website, and believe me, I checked them all. So, here are the main symptoms of perimenopause. I'll tell you what I have, and you can check it against yourselves.

1. Hot flashes and/or night sweats

Luckily, I don't have the hot flashes yet. But I do have the night sweats. (Addendum—since I wrote this a couple of months ago, I've been inundated with hot flashes.) It's wild. I'm going along doing whatever, la la la la la, and then suddenly, I'm on fire. It's like spontaneous combustion with no rhyme or reason to it. I'm not a sweater, but now, several times a day, I'm drenched. I say to Jimmy, "Feel the back of my neck." And he invariably responds, "Honey, I felt it an hour ago." He doesn't seem to be as fascinated with my fluctuating body temperature as I am. The night sweats have increased. I wake up every few hours in a pool of fluid and not the good kind. I'll have the A/C set to Ice Station Zebra and still my body is hot and clammy. Jimmy wanting to touch me in those moments is not a good idea. As a matter of fact, it's an act punishable by death. The last thing you want when your body feels like it's in the middle of Dante's inferno is to be touched. And I think there's an adrenaline rush too, because once you're up, it's impossible to get back to sleep. My heart and head are racing a mile a minute.

2. Trouble sleeping

See number 1. I've been awake since November 25, 2006. But I do know how to buy real estate with no money down. So you've got to take the good with the bad. Besides, I get a lot of work done in those wee hours of the morning. Not meaning-

ful work, but I keep busy. My files have never been so orga-
nized and my liquor cabinet never so bare.

3. Vaginal dryness

Although I know that male readers are now closing the book
and heading to the plasma TV, I must persist and address it. If
we have to deal with it, then so do you. This symptom annoys
the shit out of me. Who wants a dry, crusty vagina? Not me.
As of this writing, mine is still moist and delightful, thank
you very much. It's like a vaginal wetlands down there. Jimmy
Hoffa may be buried in my vagina, for all I know. To me, KY
still means Kentucky. But for how long? Will I wake up one
day and have to file a drought report? Is it in my future? I ask
my postmenopausal friends and some of them say they have
it and others say not. Are they lying? Some tell me that they
don't have dryness, but rather a thinning of the vaginal walls.
What the fuck is that? It doesn't sound like something I have
any interest in. What's behind those walls? And how thin does
it get? Can it disappear altogether? Should I call Bob Vila in to
build an addition? So many questions and so few answers. I'll
have to wait and see. But one thing I know for sure, I'd rather
have vaginal dryness than erectile dysfunction. At least with
the dryness you can use a lubricant or salve and maybe it gets
a little drippy but it's all external and harmless. With erectile
dysfunction, however, you have to take a pill that screws with
your biology, and there are all sorts of side effects. The four-
hour erection, for example. The thought of anyone—even
Clive Owen, hot as he is—coming after me for four hours is
frightening. The thought of Bob Dole, packin' wood, on the

prowl . . . I don't even want to think about it. It's too disturbing. I wouldn't know what the hell to do with it for four hours. Four minutes is about my limit. Besides, I don't even want to do anything that I *like* for four hours!

4. *Mood swings*

Fuck you.

I've had mood swings since I was seven. Nothing new here.

5. *Weight gain*

If I want to lose weight at this point, I have to eat absolutely nothing. I'm not exaggerating. Nothing! Recently I tried to take off this four pounds that I can't seem to get rid of, so I had 1,200 calories a day and worked out daily and I gained a pound and a half. I even cut out red wine, which is not easy for me because I enjoy my glass or two of wine at dinner, but I cut it out and still I gained weight. Can someone explain this to me? I'm thinking of drinking alcoholically, because if I'm going to keep gaining weight no matter what I do, then I might as well be hammered and not give a shit about my appearance. If I'm going to be bloated, I might as well be loaded. (Oh, and by the way, cutting out the wine did nothing to alleviate my hot flashes either, which is one of the useless pieces of advice I found online.) I used to be able to eat anything and stay thin. And then when I hit thirty that kind of ended, but I was still able to take it off when I had to. Now I gain weight eating carrots. Whatever. I don't want to make myself crazy, but truth be told, I'm making myself crazy.

6. Trouble focusing

I can't remember a goddamn thing anymore, and you know what, it's made absolutely no difference in my life. There isn't much worth remembering anyway. And if I repeat myself because I don't remember that I said it before, too bad. You'll just have to listen again. My kids roll their eyes, like anything that they have to say could be half as interesting as what I'm saying for the second or seventh time.

6. Trouble focusing

I can't remember a goddamn thing anymore, and you know what, it's made absolutely no difference in my life. There isn't much worth remembering anyway. And if I repeat myself because I don't remember that I said it before, too bad. You'll just have to listen again. My kids roll their eyes, like anything that they have to say could be half as interesting as what I'm saying for the second or seventh time.

7. Less hair on head, more on face

What is that? Less hair on head, more on face! That's almost as annoying as vaginal dryness. Actually, I think hair reassignment is worse than the dry vagina, because nobody sees your vagina in public on a regular basis, at least not mine, but your face and head are on constant display! I've seen these women with their whiskers and combovers on the streets of New York. I always thought they were mentally ill. How horrible of me. Someday I will be them. When is it going to happen? Is it slow? A whisker here, a five o'clock shadow there? Or does it happen all at once so that by July, I'm going to look like Rob Reiner?

I don't know. There's not much I can do about any of it anyway. I guess I just have to accept the fact that I'm going to end up a bald, fat, sweaty, irritable woman with a dry vagina and a full beard, who never sleeps and has memory loss so I won't even be able to remember how hot I used to look! The only comfort I take in all this is that I'll be dead soon anyway. Hopefully heart murmurs are genetic.

My grandparents, Millie and Izzie Essman

I'm a New York Yankee fan, and I come by it honestly. My Yankee love is deeply ingrained in my psyche and is completely irrational. But that's true with most fans. That's what's so great about sports. The fandom exceeds all rational thought and instead draws on raw, base emotion.

Watching spectator sports and following a team is the single greatest distraction in life—even more than raising children, which is pretty damn distracting. Sports allow us to feel things that may be inappropriate in any other setting. We can express joy, sorrow, fear, anxiety, depression, elation, hatred, and it's all within the confines of a controlled environment. It's like therapy, only better, because it takes up more time, it costs less, and there are refreshments. I scream, I yell, I believe in curses and superstitions, I pray and I make deals with the powers above. There are entire cities and their inhabitants that I despise because they're rivals of my teams. I become completely irrational, occasionally hysterical, yet in the specter of sports, it's all socially acceptable. And I'm not being glib. I mean it. I really really hate those cities and their teams, and especially their fans. And when one of the members of their team gets traded and is now on my team, it's amazing how quickly I can rationalize their redemption, and forgive the prior atrocities they committed. I can despise an opposing team with a passion, and it only means that I'm a good and loyal fan, not a sociopath filled with hate (although one doesn't necessarily preclude the other). But the point is, no one gets hurt, unless you're one of those crazy European soccer fans. They're just nuts!

Since the days of the gladiators fighting to the death in the Coliseum (maybe even before that, but I haven't seen that show on the History Channel yet), spectator sports have always had mass appeal. Daniel, in the lions' den? Huge turnout.

Experiencing the thrill of victory and the agony of defeat is like having sex—it's much more fun when other people are involved. Being a fanatic is more satisfying if you're doing it with other fanatics. You're kindred spirits and the fact that you're not crazy is affirmed by hundreds of thousands of people doing the same crazy thing you're doing. You belong to something. You understand one another's pain, sorrow, and glee. And there's always something to watch and talk about endlessly. In every season, there's something to follow—pennant races, trades, statistics, and, of course, gossip. I love dish about athletes. Much more interesting than gossip about actors, because who are actors anyway? They just say lines that other people wrote, but athletes are performing heroic feats. And so many of them are hunky, gorgeous men! It's a field day for us women. As I said, it's the ultimate distraction. The world may be falling apart, but I always turn to the sports section first.

I'm a football fan (Go Giants!), but baseball is my first love. It's a long season and there's constant drama: ups and downs and streaks and records, endless entertainment for six whole months, seven if you're lucky. In baseball, things can change so quickly; you're never safe. Your team is seven and a half games back and then ten days later they're leading their division or vice versa. Your ace pitcher gets injured and some kid comes up from the minors and wows the world (or not).

As a rule, baseball players' behavior on the field seems far more dignified and less ridiculous than athletes who play other sports. Derek Jeter is a prime example of this (of course Derek Jeter is a prime example of a lot of things, all of them good, but more on that later). You don't see Jeter sticking his tush in the air and doing a little jig when he lands on home plate, like a football player in the end zone. And don't even get me started on the histrionics of hockey players. They are so silly and primal.

Maybe it's because baseball is not a contact sport and there's no race with the clock that makes it so elegant. The pace gives the athletes time to think. It's reactive, but thoughtful. Like tennis, which I also love, every point hard won, mano a mano, but the team dynamics make baseball a more intricate game. Each player relies on the performance of his teammates to achieve victory. A pitcher may pitch a great game, but if his teammates don't hit or field, he'll lose. Baseball has so much more to absorb and follow, and so many games to distract.

Every October, I sit shiva, mourning the end of the season, and wait, counting the days until the pitchers and catchers report for spring training in February. Got nothing to do on a Tuesday night in June? There's a baseball game on, and millions of people are watching along with you. You're not so alone after all.

I first became interested in sports—football, mostly—as a way to bond with my father. It was a neutral area for us. A place we could connect and be on the same side. We had a volatile relationship, and sports were our safe zone. Instead of fighting, we could be in complete agreement and understanding. Watching sports with my father was my peaceful time. Even when I got older and moved out of the house, he and I'd watch together over the phone. He'd call seven or eight times on a Sunday during a Giants game. His need to connect with me was as powerful as my need to connect with him.

My father was a nationally ranked fencer. He parried and lunged his way onto the U.S. Olympic team but had to bow out due to a bout of hepatitis. Actually, I'm not sure if that's the exact truth, but that's what I remember, so I'm sticking with it. Every family has their myths, and that was one of ours. Daddy could have won an Olympic medal if only things had been different. Not going to the Olympics was the great disappointment of his life. His best friend won the bronze medal the year he dropped out—1960—and was the first American to ever medal in the sport; my dad used to beat him frequently in matches. Now, that's not to say that he would have won a medal himself had he gone, but the possibility had always been lurking. He could have been a contender, although I wouldn't exactly say he ended up a bum. He was a highly respected doctor, an internist with a subspecialty in oncology. He worked hard, and when he came home after a stressful day of dealing with death, he'd escape by burying his head in the newspaper; on the weekends, in sports.

Oddly enough, even though Dad was an athlete, I don't remember him ever encouraging any of us kids to take up sports. In fact, he didn't really get involved in any of our endeavors—athletic or otherwise. I don't think he ever even went to one of my brother's Little League games. Maybe it was lack of time, or the stress of his work—we'll never know—but how sad is that? My mother had to pick up the slack, so we tended to get more involved in artistic pursuits because those were her interests. She was educated and cultured, and in the long run, the things she encouraged and exposed us to served me well, because I certainly wasn't going to be a professional badminton player. Mom took me and my brother and sisters to Broadway plays, the ballet, museums, Leonard Bernstein's Young People's Concerts, and movies. The first time I ever went to the movies was when my mother took me to a revival house in Greenwich Village to see a double bill of *Singing in the Rain* and *On the Town*. I was five years old and awestruck. But still, I needed to find some area of common ground with my father.

I saw an opportunity and jumped on it. In life, we take what we can. It wasn't a conscious thing, but I'd sit with him while he was watching football and ask questions because I was interested and slowly began to understand the game and like it. My father loved to play the knowledgeable professor, and the thing about sports is, the more you understand it, the more you get the nuances and subtleties of the game—the more you enjoy it. He taught me an appreciation of the players and the game, the strategy, the beauty of athleticism, the competitiveness, the probabilities, the faith, the mysticism.

My father and I were New York Giants fans. Fandom is something we're born into. It's passed on through generations as a result of chance geography or some vague, incidental connection. Your grandfather once met the quarterback or was related to the linebacker's second cousin by marriage. That's all it took for a lifetime of devotion.

Basketball became a passion, because I went to high school in Mt. Vernon, New York, which at that time had the number one basketball team in the state—the Mt. Vernon Knights. They were incredible. My high school years also coincided with the great, classic years of the New York Knicks. Basketball love was pervasive and contagious. Do you know how much fun it is to attend a high school with a nationally ranked team? The senses of those games are so vivid and memorable to me. I can still hear the sounds of sneakers squeaking on the gym floor and feel the instability of climbing up and down the rickety bleachers, and the smell and taste of the menthol cigarette (we smoked it because the menthol got us high) my boyfriend and I used to share outside at halftime. I remember the cheers the cheerleaders performed, right down to their choreography:

Ungowa, Knight power,
Knights are the best.
Hit 'em in the chest.
What you gonna do?
Dance the boogaloo.
C stands for can.
D stands for do.
Us the mighty Knights
are gonna sock it to you.
Hey, hey, hey sock it to you.

And then they went into some frenzied foot-stomping routine that shook the whole gym. We're so fragile as teenagers that the pride and self-esteem of a high school sports team can have a long-term effect on you even as a spectator.

So I learned basketball from a high school boyfriend and football from my dad—but baseball, my first love, I learned from my grandfather. I don't remember my father ever watching baseball. I think it was too slow for him and not enough contact. He was a fencer after all, which is all about battle. Football was a better fit. He grew up a poor kid of uneducated immigrant parents on the Lower East Side of Manhattan, and at fifteen or sixteen he wandered into the Henry Street Settlement (a community center for immigrant families) where, by chance, he took up fencing. I believe it saved his life at the time as sports do for a lot of lost and angry adolescent boys. It was a place to go, a place to do something he could be good at. He had a mentor, something he didn't have in his own father, and a place to put all that competitive energy that he had so much of.

My father was an intellectual and an autodidact. He never graduated high school because he was kicked out for truancy. But he wasn't out on the streets or home watching TV, like I was when I cut school. He spent the entire day at the library reading everything imaginable—from chemistry textbooks to novels. When he was drafted into the army during World War II, he was given an IQ test and scored high. The army sent him through six months of premed and then to medical school. Who knows who or what he would have become if that happy accident hadn't happened to him. He was a high school dropout who never went to college, but because it was wartime and rules were bent, he went straight to medical school and became an oncologist. He was a remarkable man who loved to read and learn and instilled in me a love of books that I will always appreciate. I don't know where he got his love of learning, because it wasn't something that he saw at home.

His parents weren't ambitious for their children, as so many Jewish parents of his generation were. They didn't emphasize education or make sure their kids had a better life than they did. They just weren't aware of those things. They had hard lives and focused on survival. One of the reasons my father ignored his kids is that as a kid his parents didn't interact much with him. Experience is the greatest teacher, and what my father experienced at home was neglect. It wasn't out of malice or disinterest; he just never received recognition and didn't understand a child's need for love and affection and attention.

My grandmother, Millie Essman, was extremely loving but also emotionally limited by her own experiences. She left school in the third grade to work in her father's bakery and then worked in a button factory her entire adult life. Her love-less marriage with my grandfather was arranged when she was eighteen years old. My grandfather, Izzie Essman, took on whatever odd jobs he could find and was an occasional taxi driver, janitor, and, in his later years, elevator operator—a union job. (His stint as the elevator operator was poignant. My grandfather was the oldest of five brothers and the only one who was not successful. He operated the elevator in a building one of his younger brothers owned; it housed his successful manufacturing company. The younger brother gave his older brother the menial job of running the elevator.) Grandpa wasn't particularly motivated, plus he liked to gamble, so there went the little money he did manage to make. My grandmother was the one with the brains and the sense of humor, but she was beaten down by life and circumstance.

My father and his father were as different as two people could be. Grandpa Izzie was simple. The story the family likes to tell is that he got hit on the head as a child and was never the same after that. He was a bit of an idiot savant because he was clearly not that bright but had an incredible memory for things like sports stats. My grandparents had a very unhappy marriage. My grandfather had a twin brother who died in infancy. My grandmother used to shout at her husband, "Izzie, the wrong twin died!" Nice, huh? I guess that's what having no options in life does to a person.

When I was a kid my grandparents lived on Jerome Avenue in the Bronx, right across the street from Yankee Stadium. It was like the Taj Mahal, nestled between the Major Deegan Expressway and the elevated subway tracks. I used to sit on the fire escape of my grandparents' apartment and stare at the stadium while Grandpa Izzie had the game on TV. He always had the baseball game on TV. It was a constant hum in the background, and the games seemed to go on forever. He'd have loud, heated, one-sided arguments with the players on the screen. He knew all about them and would reel off stats about each. He didn't seem mentally deficient to me. As a matter of fact, he was a wealth of baseball knowledge, and whether he knew it or not, he was teaching me about the game and nurturing my love of it.

I loved visiting my grandparents in the Bronx. I used to go for the weekend and sleep on the pull-out couch in the living room. My brother and sister never wanted to go, so it was just me and Grandma and Grandpa. They had a one-bedroom apartment with an efficiency kitchen that reeked of old people. The elderly have very distinct smells, not all of them bad. My grandparents' apartment had the smell of Eastern Europe packed up and transplanted, and stale lives almost over. I loved that smell.

Grandpa Izzie always had a little gift for me. When I got to his apartment he'd go to the top drawer of his dresser and pull out treasures that he'd found on the streets and washed and cleaned and wrapped in tissue paper. You couldn't find this stuff in the pristine suburbs of Westchester, where there wasn't any street life, but the Bronx was full of hidden treasures. Grandpa Izzie was like a scavenger scouring the streets for things that people lost or foolishly discarded. He'd spot things from a block away. He was amazing at finding crap, like he had a special Geiger counter implanted in his brain.

There were Cracker Jack toys, key chains, broken pieces of jewelry, lots of pink Spalding balls, marbles, religious medals of varied denominations, broken cigarette lighters, and an object that I still have in my jewelry box—a chainless, gold-plated ID bracelet that has *Charles* on the front and *Love, Marjorie* engraved on the back. The Bronx was a treasure trove, and everywhere you looked was baseball. Kids playing Little League in the park next to the stadium, stickball games on the side streets, and, of course, the grand palace dominating the landscape.

Grandma Millie and I used to wake up in the morning and walk the streets to take care of the day's errands. We walked everywhere, the stadium always my guidepost. We'd stop at four different supermarkets and price everything out before making purchases. Grandma Millie had a mind like a steel trap and remembered how much each store charged per pound for every item on the list in her head.

I aquired my love of walking the streets of New York from Millie and Izzie. (As opposed to my love of streetwalking, which I acquired from a miniskirted transvestite named Glen.) The streets of New York were always alive, always something to look at, always people around. Nothing boring or dull and magnificent structures and boulevards everywhere I turned. Sometimes we'd travel by subway, and my grandmother amazed me because she knew her way around underground. It was all a great adventure. You know how on Christmas you'll buy some really expensive toy for a toddler and all she wants to play with is the box it came in? That's how I felt about the Bronx. I lived there until I was three, when we moved to Mt. Vernon in Westchester. Geographically it was right next to the Bronx but environmentally and culturally, they were worlds apart. I lived in a big beautiful house on a tree-lined street and had a big backyard with swings, but I preferred the cramped quarters and bustling streets of the Bronx. It's one of the reasons I never moved to L.A.—too suburban. I like street life. I thrive on it.

Grandma Millie was my favorite person in the world. I

adored her. She was effortlessly funny—she had that natural survival-mode humor that likely carried her through a mostly disappointing life. Humor was in her bones. She spent the last years of her life in a nursing home, completely senile with no idea who she or anybody else was, yet when I'd visit her, the West Indian nurses would tell me that she had them laughing all day long. She'd lost everything—her mind, her dignity, her identity—but she held onto her sense of humor. I'd like to think that some day, if I become hunched, decrepit, and talk to furniture, I'll still be able to find a punch line and deliver it with perfect timing and style.

I remember the last thing Grandma Millie ever said to me. I was visiting her in the home, and she didn't know who I was. I was trying to snap her back to reality by asking her questions. Why, I don't know, because she clearly was happier and calmer in dementia. When she was aware, she was in despair and agitated and begged me to get her out of there. Her not knowing me was painful, and I wanted my Grandma back. It was selfish, and I should have left her alone in her delusional state. But how could I let my grandmother abandon me and let this feeble old woman inhabit her body without at least attempting to keep alive the woman I knew and loved and desperately needed?

On this day, she looked up at me with those beautiful hazel eyes that had gone dull. The twinkle she'd always managed to maintain in spite of her difficult ninety years was gone. "How old are you, Granny?" I blurted out, thinking I'd get her brain churning and she'd snap back to reality. Staring at me, the twinkle returned momentarily, and she said derisively, "Kish mir en toches," which means *Kiss my ass* in Yiddish. I laughed because it was so like her, and of course she was right—it was a stupid question! I knew exactly how old she was, and at that point, who cared anyway? Then she started to moan, "Everything changes, everything changes, everything changes" over and over again. It was very Zen. My grandmother, whom I'm sure didn't know what Zen or Buddhism was, and whose philosophical readings extended as far as the homilies in *Reader's Digest,* was a Zen master. Those last words, "Kiss my ass. Everything changes," have become my legacy. Let everything go, but hold onto your sense of humor.

Grandma Millie languished, became vegetative, and eventually died. I still miss her, and when I go to Yankee Stadium I look for her in the streets of the Bronx.

It was after both my grandparents died that I returned to baseball. I had abandoned my interest in it for a while and football had taken over, but the beauty of baseball was pulling me back in. There was a group of male comics that I spent a lot of time with, and they sat at the bar of the Comic Strip and talked baseball. Yogi Berra, another Zen master, once said, "In baseball you don't know nuthin'." Baseball as a metaphor began to gradually resonate with me, and my old Yankee love was slowly kindled. Maybe it was nostalgia for my lost childhood spent in the Bronx with my grandparents, but it was auspicious, because it was the early '90s and just a few years before the great Yankee teams would dominate the sport. It's so much easier to follow and love a winning team than a losing one! And it was fortunate for another reason, because without the Yankees, I don't know how I would have gotten through one of the most difficult times of my life.

In the summer of 2001, my father was dying after a two-and-a-half-year battle with esophageal cancer. Whatever anyone tells you about the horrors of drawn-out cancer deaths—it's worse. By the end of his life, my big, strong, tough daddy was a frail eighty-five pounds. I watched him wither away for months, until on August 25, he died. Mostly I just sat with him either at home, in the hospital, or in the convalescence facility. There wasn't much else to do. He was in and out of the hospital all summer. At night, I'd go home and watch the Yankees. It was the only thing that distracted me. I'd zone out, have a glass of wine, be a spectator, and wait for the next phone call. I'd begun to dread the sound of the phone ringing. Over and over, it would ring and be my mother or my sisters telling me Dad was in the emergency room again. He needed a feeding tube, the feeding tube was infected; he needed a stent, the stent had to be removed; it was endless. One time, after he'd collapsed, I had to literally carry him down the stairs of his house and bring him to the emergency room myself, watching him die in the rearview mirror as I drove. And time after time, he'd miraculously bounce back, until it became clear that he wouldn't. There's a certain relief when you're no longer waiting for the call because, well, you're no longer waiting for the call. You can finally sleep through the night.

Over those last few months, it was a privilege to watch my father die. At some point in life, children watch their parents die, and hopefully never the other way around. As sad as it was, there was something enlightening about seeing the process. It's the natural order of things.

The day before my dad died I cut his hair and sat with him for a few hours. He was hallucinating, and I could feel his essence leaving his body. He was getting so wispy. And when he died the next day and I stood over his lifeless form, I stared at him, and his body was just that—a vessel, a carrier, a borrowed container. I think it's important to see the dead person before they gussy it up for the funeral and try to make them look alive, if not festive (although my dad would have none of that and requested cremation). But when we see the dead body, it's very clear that the person is indeed gone. It's palpable. Death is so shocking, even when we're prepared for it. It's so final.

A few months before my father's death, a cousin of ours who was in his thirties committed suicide. A few weeks before my father's death, two acquaintances of mine died—one from lupus and the other from a brain hemorrhage. Death was in the air, and I was becoming familiar with grief. A week after Dad's death, a childhood friend was killed in a car accident, and then two weeks to the day after his funeral was 9/11.

The two events became indelibly linked in my brain. For an entire year, the only images I saw when I closed my eyes were my father's dead body and the two planes crashing into the twin towers. It was a horrible time. Anyone who lived in Manhattan remembers what it was like in those days after the attack. It was surreal, almost like being in a David Lynch movie, except there were no closing credits—it just kept going on and on. We were all traumatized. I remember walking around and feeling the pain of the city and thinking, *Everyone feels like I've been feeling for the past two weeks, only worse.* It was a collective mourning that was so touching and all-pervasive. The most noticeable thing was the silence. For days, the streets and the people walking them made virtually no sound, but it didn't feel eerie; it felt appropriate. We all felt quiet and anguished, injured and stunned. There was a big, gaping hole in our city. A big festering wound throbbing with pain.

Everywhere we looked were flyers with the faces of the missing. They were posted all over the city. After a couple of days, it became clear that none of those faces were going to miraculously show up; they weren't missing, they were gone. Every one of those people had perished, and it was hard to wrap our heads around that kind of devastation. Especially since it was brought upon us by fellow human beings. A good friend of a good friend was in the burn unit at Cornell Medical Center. She'd been hit by a fireball of jet fuel in the lobby of one of the towers and had third-degree wounds over three-quarters of her body. She was one of the few survivors and in a coma. They identified her by her feet—her face was unrecognizable. Mercifully, she died five weeks later, but it was a long five weeks.

Everyone either knew someone who died or knew someone who knew someone. It was two degrees of separation. No one was unaffected.

There are very few things in life that I love more than the city of New York. I've loved it through thick and thin, for richer for poorer. I took those attacks—like so many New

Yorkers did—personally. I felt helpless and angry. New York is my home. I'm connected to everything and everyone that lives here. We're all a part of the collective unconscious of the place, and we all collectively grieved and mourned. How were we ever going to collectively heal?

I didn't know how I would ever get back onstage. What could I possibly say that would be funny? After about three weeks, the calls and requests to do benefits started coming in. There were benefits all over the city. That's what we do in New York when we're grieving—we find ways to connect to one another. We're a city filled with people. Millions of us walk the same crowded streets every day and figure out how to navigate and get along. We had to pull together and at least make small steps toward normalcy and healing. I had to get back onstage and try and make people laugh. It felt like my duty. I must have done two dozen benefits for firemen alone. I was needed, and in truth—I needed to be needed. Besides, I was consumed with rage, and there was no better place to put it than on the stage. I did what I could, however small, as did everyone. We were all in this together. We were going to get through it together.

And then there were those noble, always-there-in-the-clutch Yankees. If ever a city needed a distraction, it was New York in the fall of 2001. The Yankees gave us focus and a reason to feel joyful again. And once again, we were all in it together. Every last one of us Yankee fans and maybe even some reluctant Mets fans too. The healing would only come collectively. The individual work wasn't enough. We had to feel the force of the crowd. We had something else to talk about, pay attention to, and cheer for when it felt like there would never be anything to cheer for again.

The 2001 play-offs were utterly electric. I couldn't wait for the games. Lived for them. From Derek Jeter's game-saving flip into Posada's catcher's mitt in game three of the first series against Oakland to beating the Mariners, who had the best record in baseball at that time. Let me take this opportunity to say that I'm in love with Derek Jeter (I told you I'd get to this). My husband Jimmy understands that he's the only man I'd cheat on him for, and he's okay with it. Mostly because he knows that the likelihood of that happening is next to nothing. In fact, if Jimmy wanted to cheat on me with Derek Jeter, I'd be okay with that too. And it's not just that Jeter is so attractive; it's all the other stuff—the professionalism, the way he conducts himself on and off the field, the way he's always there in the clutch, always taking full responsibility. I could go on. He's the consummate player and he has fun—always smiling and laughing and having the greatest time. He's the Fred Astaire of baseball, working his ass off and making it all look so elegant and easy. There's nothing I enjoy more than watching Jeter catch a ball midair and then pivot and fire to first base. It's a thing of beauty and an image that I carry with me. It makes me happy.

So the Yanks got to the 2001 World Series. Winning wasn't a fait accompli as it had been in previous years, although it never really is in any sport, with too many variables like injury and luck. They had some stiff competition. But we needed them to go on. We needed to stay focused on something other than grief, and that something was our glorious New

York baseball team. We weren't anywhere near healed and we wouldn't be for years, if ever, but we needed more from the Yankees, and they literally stepped up to the plate. How could we have watched some other city's team for those last weeks of October? New York deserved a better spotlight.

The Yankees gave the city everything we needed and then some. They gave us miracles. They were down two games to one in the World Series 'against the Arizona Diamondbacks. And then in games four and five at Yankee Stadium they hit a home run when they were down to their last out and trailing by two runs. Twice! Two nights in a row! And of course, one of the homers was hit by my fantasy man, Derek Jeter. It was unbelievable. I cried my eyes out at both games. Relief, joy, sadness all rolled into one. It's everything that I love about sports. The glory, the personal triumphs, the unpredictability, the heart and soul of the thing.

That's not to say that the Yankees could have ever made up for the grief and loss we all felt, but they gave us something important nonetheless. It was sheer perfection of a series, even down to the seventh-game, ninth-inning loss, on a run given up by Mariano Rivera, of all people (a god among men). We lost the series and maybe that's the way it should've been. I don't know if we could have taken a win—if we were ready to celebrate. A ticker tape parade in downtown Manhattan was unthinkable under the circumstances. Personally, I felt the Yankees did New York a favor by losing. I'm sure George Steinbrenner disagrees. But in that moment, on that night in November, almost two months since I watched my father die, almost two months since the World Trade Center went down in flames, almost two months since my city was sent into a tailspin of grief and mourning, in the shadows of the smoke of lower Manhattan, the Yankees gave me and the entire city a distraction up until the very last out, and that was about all we could handle. It was enough. I was grateful to them, and to my father and my grandfather—grateful for my love of the game.

CHAPTER
8

*THE
ALBANIAN WAY*

When I was in my twenties, a guy I knew told me that in his writings, Casanova made a reference to having sex "the Albanian Way." Casanova never indicated exactly what "The Albanian Way" was, but it was supposed to be the ultimate sexual thrill for women. I was suspicious that there really was any such thing because (a) the guy who told me this was Albanian and hitting on me and (b) the only Albanian woman I could think of was Mother Teresa. Still, it made me wonder, was there some sexual information out there that I wasn't privy to? Did other people know things that I didn't?

I remember the bad girls in ninth grade. At fifteen, they were already women. They dressed like women, they looked like women, and they were having sex like women. Or so it seemed. They went out with older guys, wore flesh-toned nylons and lots of makeup, and had outdated hairdos. They were the girls with reputations and had nicknames like Roundheels or BJ or The Mattress. They clearly knew a lot of things that I didn't. We were in the same grade, but definitely not in the same class. They were already women and I was still a little girl. They were Sophia Loren, and I was Pippi Longstocking.

The following summer, when I was going into tenth grade, my best friend told me that she'd given her boyfriend a hand job. I was appalled and completely grossed out. How could she even touch it, let alone touch it to . . . fruition? Only a week before, my boyfriend of the week had tried to place my hand ever so indelicately down his pants and had soon realized that there had not even been a remote possibility of that happening. I think my clenched fist and projectile vomiting had been dead giveaways. Of course a short year later my attitude toward sex inevitably changed. I became curious and it didn't seem gross to me anymore. In fact, the thought of it went from appalling to appealing. Yet I still didn't seem to know what the bad girls knew. They were still Sophia Loren, but now I was Audrey Hepburn. (Audrey, who was always beloved by women and gay men, apparently did nothing for hetero males.)

As I got older and became sexually active (I've always hated that expression, "sexually active"; it makes my vagina sound like a volcano or a geyser or some natural disaster), I thought that everyone was having better sex than I was. Well, not everyone. Not Richard Nixon, for example. But someone out there was having absolutely magnificent sex and they knew things that I couldn't even imagine. Some secret, some wisdom of the ages, some Playboy Bunny-defying position . . . something that made whatever kind of sex I was having seem bland and pedestrian. And I know this because my friends and I would compare notes and invariably, their sex always sounded so much better no matter how good the sex I was having was. Even when I had what I considered *really* great sex, someone always made their sex sound even more interesting and exciting. Did everyone feel that way, or was it just me?

Not that you should ever believe anything that people tell

you about their sex lives. People lie about this all the time and I've never understood why. Do they think I'm so shallow that I would use their sexual exploits as the measuring stick of their worth as human beings? Okay, let's say I would; am I supposed to be impressed that your penis bends three feet to the left, or that you gave head to an entire traveling circus in less than an hour? I had a friend in college who was notorious for raving about the sex she had with each successive short-lived boyfriend. I was envious every time, and then they'd break up and the truth would come out. Stuff like he never got fully erect or he thought receiving oral sex was slimy and disgusting or he could only get turned on by listening to Walter Cronkite deliver the evening news. Years later she finally admitted that she wasn't even orgasmic in those days. Still, at the time, I was sure she knew something that I didn't. (Turns out that she did—she knew how to lie.)

I was in total despair, convinced that I would never find the key that unlocked that magic box, and for the rest of my life inspired sexual satisfaction would remain as much of a mystery to me as the conclusions of the Warren Commission and my aunt Shirley's uncanny ability to eat an entire eight-pound capon in one sitting. But then, one day, out of the blue—BOOM! I turned thirty-five and suddenly, miraculously, I knew. It was *that* simple. What was the big secret? Well, it wasn't to be found in the Kama Sutra, the latest *Cosmo* quiz, or the letters of Eleanor Roosevelt. The answer was, as Dorothy learned in Oz, inside of me the whole time. It's the hormones, stupid! Women begin their sexual peak in their midthirties. That's just a fact. Why? I have no idea. It doesn't make a lot of sense in the evolutionary scheme of things, but since I'm not having sex with Darwin, I don't really care. All I know is, once you hit it, hold on tight, because it's a long ride that just gets better and better and better. I'm still not Sophia Loren, but what does she know? She's not even Albanian.

CHAPTER
9

THE BUSINESS
OF COMEDY,
PART TWO—

NEUROTIC
NEEDS, HEALTHY
RESPONSES

I n the beginning of my career, when I first put my stage
act together, I performed as various characters. Before I
was "Susie Essman," I was the people I saw and heard on
the bus; members of my family; a Hispanic girl I over-
heard in the bathroom of a club one night; my friend Lisa's
grandmother, who used to sell hot clothing from her apartment in Co-op City in the Bronx; customers at the restaurant;
a black radical activist; a sex therapist; a Greenwich, Connecticut wasp. Either I was a comic or a schizophrenic. I'd either
get laughs or paper slippers. I never spoke in my own voice,
and after about six weeks, I started doing little intros to the
characters. Paul and Burt were giving me spots regularly at
Comedy U, and I was feeling more and more comfortable. By
early 1984, after about four months of regularly performing,
when it became clear (at least to me) that I was going to do
this, that I was going to pursue a career as a stand-up comic, I
realized that I had to start developing my own character, my
own persona as a comic.

People always ask me about my stand-up comedy influences,
especially the women. I didn't really have any. I loved watching Phyllis Diller, Totie Fields, Joan Rivers, and Anne Meara
on the *Ed Sullivan Show,* or the *Tonight Show.* They were hilarious but I never thought, *I'd like to do what they're doing.* I
saw myself as Eve Arden, not Jackie Mason. I was going to be
a character actress, not a jokester.

I wasn't a comedy aficionado and I didn't frequent comedy clubs. As a matter of fact, the only time I had even been in a comedy club before I actually performed in one was in 1982. I was visiting Los Angeles and I saw Richard Pryor at The Comedy Store. He was onstage workshopping new material. Some of it worked and some of it didn't. He was obviously brilliant, but I never knew that comics worked like that. I never knew that they went up onstage and actually worked through material in front of a live audience. When I saw them on TV they would stand there and tell jokes or do bits and it frequently seemed contrived. Pryor worked differently. He was a real person, not some made-up character. He seemed like he was actually having a conversation with the audience, not spitting out preconceived and rehearsed lines.

After I started doing stand-up, I rented the tape of Pryor's 1979 concert film. It was illuminating. It was the first time I watched a comedian and thought, *I want to be doing what he's doing.* He was everything I thought a comic should be, and I was none of those things. Not yet at least. He was funny, but a lot of people are funny. The difference with Pryor was that he was real and vulnerable and raw and accessible. Through stories and jokes and characters, he told the truth, and he wasn't afraid of exposing ugly things about himself. He was warm and loving and loveable. He had it all.

There were many comics I admired when I was in my teens and twenties. I'd never miss a Woody Allen or Mel Brooks film, or David Steinberg or Don Rickles on the *Tonight Show,* but once I became a comedian, it was Pryor whom I wanted to emulate most. I connected with Richard Pryor in a way that only a middle-class, suburban, Jewish woman can connect with a drug-addled, inner-city black man. In Richard Pryor, I saw something of myself.

The other comic who had a great influence on me both professionally and personally was Joy Behar. When we first met, backstage at Comedy U, in 1984, I was living in a minuscule fourth-floor walk-up in Manhattan and she was a divorced, single mother and unemployed schoolteacher, living in a one-bedroom apartment in Queens with her thirteen-year-old daughter.

Joy was the same person onstage as she was off—she was herself. Yes, onstage she had material and timing, but her persona had no contrivance to it. So many of the comics I'd seen in those first few months working in clubs seemed like they were trying to perform their idea of what a "comic" should sound like. Not Joy. I remember watching her and thinking, *Oh, I get it. She's just Joy. Like she's sitting around talking to her friends.* Right then I knew that I didn't have to change who I already was or figure out who I wanted to be. I was already funny, so I just had to be myself.

Easier said than done. Joy has a gift for being herself. And that's not to say that she didn't work really hard on becoming a great comic. She did, she does, and she is. There are so many different aspects of being a comedian, but Joy's voice, her comedic persona, was present from the beginning. You can learn how to write material, construct a joke, or put an act together, but you can't learn persona.

I knew who I was with my friends, but how could I be that way in a room full of strangers? Onstage, I spoke in other people's voices, became other characters. How could I find my own voice and be my own character? How could I bring off-stage Susie onstage? I asked the guys at Comedy U, still the only club I was working, if I could emcee.

They said (and rightly so) that they didn't think it would work because I performed characters and as an emcee you had to shmooze the audience and get them ready for each act. I couldn't just go out and do one of my pieces and bring the next act on. It wouldn't work. I asked them to let me try. They did. Those guys, Paul and Burt, were so great. They were all about developing and nurturing talent.

I like pressure—not myocardial, but I have always worked best with a gun to my head. The first night I emceed I wrote some material in my own voice and I also tried to talk to the audience. I remember asking a guy sitting up front where he was from. "Texas," he replied. "Oh." I said. Witty, huh? I couldn't think of any retort. My brain froze. I've always been quick, but being quick onstage in front of people, people I did not know, did not come naturally to me. (Ironic in the sense that improvisation and working the room is what I've since become known for, and these days, when young comics ask me about how to work the audience, they never believe me when I tell them that I was horrible at it in the beginning—it took a lot of work, a lot of tolerating failure.) I was bad. But the only way to become a good comic is to be willing to first be bad. It's humiliating. You stand up in front of people and have no idea what you're doing, and the only way to get experience and know what you're doing is to just do it.

Eventually, I learned how to relax and just be. I don't know exactly how long it took. I'm still learning. But at some point, about three years in, I lost my self-consciousness onstage. I got up over and over and over again. I'd have good sets, I'd have bad ones, and occasionally really bad ones. Those were hard to recover from, but I had to get up the next night and get that bad taste out of my mouth. It lingered still, but I had to keep going. The bad sets always stay with you longer than the good ones. You learn more from them too.

Little by little I began to venture out to other clubs. Comedians that I met at Comedy U would tell me about a club here or there where I could get stage time. In June 1984 I auditioned at the Comic Strip. It was a Friday afternoon and I had to get onstage in an empty room in front of Lucien Hold, the creative director of the club. No audience, no waitresses, not even a wayward delivery man passing through the room, with a hand truck full of whatever; just Lucien and me. There are no laughs in an empty room. Your timing and rhythm are completely thrown. It's awkward and weird, and I felt terribly self-conscious, like there were a thousand eyes staring at me instead of none. Well, two exactly—Lucien's, and according to rumor, they were harsh and unforgiving. I'd heard the horror stories about Lucien. That he'd made some people audition ten times before he'd pass them. Some he never passed at all, and he had no problem telling them that they weren't funny and why. Luckily I wasn't one of those people, and somehow, despite the awkwardness of the situation, I did well enough to be asked to come back the following Monday night to audition in front of a live audience. I passed that audition as well, but passing was only the beginning. It didn't guarantee you stage time, it just allowed you to put in your availability for stage time.

I was thrilled to have passed at the Comic Strip, but actually getting spots onstage was a whole other ball game. There were a limited number of spots available and an unlimited number of comedians who wanted them: good comedians and not-so-good comedians; comedians with credits, comedians without credits; comedians who had been around for a long time and expected a certain loyalty from the clubs they had put time and effort into; comedians who were brilliantly funny but had not yet found their niche; comedians who were audience pleasers but had no originality and would make a living on the road but never have a career; and comedians like me—young, eager, and striving to break through. Mostly, there were male comedians. Lots and lots of them, who, for the most part, didn't want to think that women were funny.

In spite of the groundbreaking brilliance of Totie and Phyllis and Joan and Lily, comedy in those days was still very much a man's game. The comic misogyny was palpable. Thank God for Joy. We had become fast friends, and together we posed a united front that made it easier to deal with the macho bullshit thrown at us—onstage and off. There were male comics who were female friendly and there were boys who let female comics into their circle, but by and large, it was a boys' club from top to bottom. (A hetero boys' club, I might add. The straight boys were no more welcoming to the gays than they were to the girls. Maybe it's because we both camped out under the same misanthropic umbrella at the boys' club bar.)

Not surprisingly, I've always found that it was the mediocre comics who were the most sexist. The good ones, the talented ones, were unthreatened and, therefore, more supportive. The clubs themselves were less discriminatory, but women definitely had to work harder to get somewhere. That was okay with me. It made me a better comic. It was annoying, but it made me better.

Passing at the Comic Strip was a coup. It would take me two more years, not for lack of trying, to become a regular at Catch A Rising Star—*the* club to be seen in at that time. That club was my nemesis. I'd get a chance to get onstage and it never went well. I was killing all over the city, but something weird happened to me in that room. It psyched me out and I couldn't crack it. There were a series of creative directors, none of them fans of mine, and none of them passed me. Finally, in 1986, there was once again a regime change, and Cynthia Coe came in as the creative director. I remember saying to Joy, "I'm just going to act as though I passed and put my availability in. I'm not going through this audition shit again." And that's what I did.

It worked, and I was finally working at Catch. At first, I got the worst spots on the show, as all new comics do. I'd get one or two a week. Usually at two o'clock in the morning on the third show on Saturday, when the only people in the audience who weren't drunk were asleep (or more often both). I was happy to have it though. I'd get a few spots for a few weeks in a row and then I'd call one day and I wouldn't be on the schedule. Oh, the paranoia! We all went through this. Had I blown it? Was I on the shit list? Whose shit list was it? Was I on everyone's shit list? Was I out? Had I done something wrong? Then the next week I'd be on again. And it wasn't just getting any spot in the lineup, there were quality spots and there were crappy spots. The "check spot," for example, is a crappy spot. That's when the check goes down on the tables and you lose the audience's attention . . . as well as your focus, confidence, and sense of safety. For my first five or six years doing stand-up, I did lots and lots of check spots—following some generic guitar act that had worked the audience into a frenzy or standing on a bar at some comedy night in a restaurant in New Jersey with a bad mic and a bunch of men screaming, "Show us your tits!"

Doing all of those check spots and late-night drunkfests made me strong. If I could command their attention when they were haggling with the other couple over who owed what, then I had to be good, but I still had so much to learn. Comedy time is different from real time. Being a comic for five or ten years meant you were still a novice. It took years to develop an act and even longer to figure out who you were onstage, and making a living was another thing altogether. I waitressed for two years before I could even marginally make a living as a comic. I used to leave the restaurant at eleven and first go out and do spots in the clubs at midnight. After about two years into it, it was time to give up my money-making security and quit waitressing. It was time to begin hustling gigs.

A not-so-quick word here about the club scene in New York in the mid 1980s. Most of the comedy clubs at that time were what were known as showcase clubs. The three major ones were the Improv, Catch A Rising Star, and the Comic Strip. Showcase clubs were just that—places where comedians went on, one after another, to hone their craft and to "showcase" their talent. Instead of money, they got stage time—which was a far more valuable commodity than cash. During the week, the comics would get cab fare as payment, something like seven bucks, which, in those days, unless you lived in Siberia, could actually buy you a taxi ride home. On the weekends, when there were three set shows, they'd get more, like forty or fifty bucks per set. There was an audition process that usually involved standing on line for hours to get a number, then returning the following day to perform for the club owner or sometimes another comedian, who would then determine if you were good enough to put in your availability to the club to hopefully get stage time. It was extremely competitive. *Extremely.* Stage time is everything to a comic. Without it, you can't do what you do and you can't get better. A comedian thrives off of live interaction. It's not something you can practice in the mirror at home with a deodorant can as a microphone and your dog as an audience. Besides, everyone knows that dogs don't laugh when you talk to them; they stare, which is cute, but the opposite of what you want from an audience.

The comedy club scene in New York was bustling in the mid '80s, and it was the goal of every comic to pass at one of these clubs, because that's where they could be seen. On any given night there would be someone in the audience from the *Tonight Show* or Letterman or the networks searching for the next sitcom star.

There were a lot of clubs in those days—Upstairs at Greene Street (my favorite place to work on a Saturday night; it was a supper club, and I could be more conversational, less punchy—it was great for developing my comic persona), The Duplex, Stand Up New York, Comedy Cellar, Caroline's (which was a headliner's club and used people like me to open for well-established acts like Jerry Seinfeld and Richard Belzer). I didn't want to go on the road. That was too scary to me, to be away from home and have to perform. I don't think I could have handled that. I needed the security of New York and family and friends. Besides, too much road work gave comics bad habits and interfered with their career. I saw lots of good comedians who spent too much time on the road and ended up hacky and losing their edge and originality. They had to water down their acts to appeal to the lowest common denominator. In New York, you didn't have to homogenize, and if you wanted to be seen by the powers that be, you had to be in New York or Los Angeles. In Los Angeles, it was even harder to get stage time. There were fewer clubs and more people with more major credits competing for the spots. If you wanted to work on your act, if you wanted to get good, if you wanted to develop—you worked in New York.

By 1987 I was an established New York club act. I performed over four hundred shows that year alone. During the week I'd usually do two sets a night, and then on Friday and Saturday, the money nights, I'd run around the city doing six or seven shows a night. We all did in the late '80s. That was our job. That was our life. Afterwards, at 3:00 or 4:00 a.m., all jacked up on adrenaline, we'd go to the diner and go over material and talk comedy. We were all focused on the business of comedy. Running around like that, from club to club, I could make three to four hundred bucks in a weekend. Not a ton of money but enough to get by. And then here and there would be a better-paying gig. A private party, a country club, a TV commercial or voice-over, a small part in a movie or TV show, a spot on one of the many stand-up shows on cable.

There were the comics who came and went, the ones who put together a tight five minutes to showcase and hopefully get a development deal with the networks, never to be heard from again. But the good ones were always focused on the work. We took our comedy very seriously. It wasn't about being famous. It was about being a great comic. We knew that there was no such thing as an "overnight sensation," and we'd have to work hard if we were going to get anywhere.

The group that I came up with is proof of that. Besides Joy there was Chris Rock, Jon Stewart, Colin Quinn, Mario Cantone, Judy Gold, Ray Romano, Lewis Black, I could go on. We all worked our asses off. There was a period of time that it seemed like Chris Rock was the backup every weekend at Catch. That meant that he sat at the bar and waited in case someone who had a scheduled spot didn't show up or was late. I did it a bunch of times too. We'd just sit there waiting, all night. I think we got paid $20 for the privilege. When I first met Colin, he was a bartender at the Comic Strip. Years later, when he hosted *Caroline's Comedy Hour,* I was on the writing staff of the show. The staff was Colin, Louis CK, Dave Attell, Jon Stewart, and me. When Jon Stewart started coming around, I thought he was brilliant, but I couldn't imagine what a network was going to do with him. He certainly wasn't your typical sitcom type. (I guess he found his niche.) My point is, we all paid our dues, and none of us took it for granted.

We took what work we could and got onstage as much as we could. It was a fun but grueling existence, and, in hindsight, quite a romantic one.

I'm always asked what comedians make me laugh. Lots of them—all the above mentioned for sure—but the comedian who has always tickled my funny bone onstage more than any other is Gilbert Gottfried. In my early years at Catch the audience didn't always appreciate his brilliance. As a matter of fact, when it was really late and the management wanted to get rid of the last few straggler customers, they'd put Gilbert up to clear the room. The audience just didn't get him and would just stare at him like he was retarded, while all the comics in the room would be laughing.

After a while, seeing so much comedy, comedians tend to watch comics and think things like *That was funny* or *Good joke* or *I wish I had thought of that* more than actually laugh. We become inured. To this day, watching Gilbert onstage can still send me into fits of hysteria. Offstage, in real life, he causes me to gasp for air. In 1992, we were both in Miami Beach shooting our *One Night Stand* half-hour specials for HBO. There were a bunch of comics shooting within a few days of one another. Gilbert and I shot ours together with the same audience. I got down there a day or two before him and ran into a sweet, aggressively not bright woman who was working on the show named . . . well, let's just call her Barbara. Before Gilbert got there, she said to me, "I dread Gilbert coming. He's always making fun of me and saying insulting things and I just don't know how to deal with his abuse." I said, "Oh, just ignore him. Don't pay any attention to him and he'll stop. He just wants a response from you." So Gilbert got to Miami and we were hanging out together after rehearsal and Gilbert said to me, "Barbara is so weird. I was doing my usual making fun of her and she just kept on saying to me over and over again in that nasal voice, 'I'm not listening to you, I'm ignoring you, I'm not paying any attention to you, I'm not listening to you, I'm ignoring you, I'm not paying any attention to you', and she wouldn't stop repeating it." I then told him how I had told her to ignore him. This fucking dumdum girl couldn't stop telling him over and over and over again that she was ignoring him. Well, we laughed so hard that I thought I was going to die. I don't know that I've ever laughed harder. I started choking. Sure, I've heard way funnier things in my life, but Gilbert just tickles my funny bone and brings out the third grader in me. To this day, seventeen years later, whenever we see each other, we automatically start saying, "I'm not listening to you, I'm ignoring you, I'm not paying any attention to you" and start laughing hysterically all over again. We never tire of it.

One of the funniest comedians working at that time was Larry David. Like Gilbert, he was a comic's comic, meaning that the comics, who were the toughest audience, knew he was brilliant even if the audience didn't always get it. When I'd emcee and Larry was on the lineup, he'd whisper to me, "Stay close" as he walked onto the stage after I announced him. He was known for getting annoyed at audiences and walking off-stage before his time was up. Once he got up, looked at them, shook his head, said, "Never mind," and walked off. I remember a night he went on late and was in the middle of some bit about a bungalow. A woman in the audience piped up, "What's a bungalow?" Larry stormed off incensed at this woman's stupidity. But more about him (a lot more) later.

In the late '80s, comedy was king in New York. People were lined up around the block to get into the clubs. It was a good time to be a working comic. It was exciting. It was fun. There was a sense of community. I'd walk into Catch A Rising Star and know everyone from Koo the Chinese busboy to the waitresses, and bartenders, and of course the comics hanging out at the bar. It was home. It was family. It was being somewhere you belonged. It was community. It was church.

Comics from the generation before mine who were already successful (though not as successful as they would eventually become) would stop by when they were in town and get onstage—Jerry Seinfeld, Paul Reiser, Roseanne Barr, Dom Irrera, Sam Kinison. Or the generation before them—Robin Williams, Richard Lewis, Billy Crystal, Richard Belzer. In the audience would be rock stars and actors and athletes and lots and lots of regular folks who wanted to laugh.

Rodney Dangerfield lived around the corner from Catch and would show up frequently and get onstage when he had to work on a spot for the *Tonight Show*. He'd meander in, sometimes in what looked like his pajamas. Rodney was always a great supporter of young comics. He'd sit with us at the bar for hours and talk comedy. One day I was home in my fourth-floor walk-up hovel and the phone rang. It was Rodney. "Essie"—that's what he called me—"it's Rodney. I just came up with a brilliant idea for your act."

Why Rodney Dangerfield was sitting around on a Tuesday afternoon thinking about my career was beyond me. But that's the way he was. He was a big, generous, loving teddy bear.

"You should be the female Andrew Dice Clay."

He then proceeded to rattle off the types of female Dice jokes I should do. He had that kind of mind. He was a master joke writer, maybe the best ever in terms of construction. I was taking notes furiously, but needless to say, the idea didn't appeal to me. First of all, I had been working really hard to find my own voice all those years, and secondly, that kind of act relied on jokes. I was never a great joke writer. Wasn't my thing. But Rodney was so excited about the idea that I went along and listened. I think it was more of an exercise for him to come up with filthy jokes from a female point of view than anything else. I never pursued the idea, but I was flattered that he thought of me. The last time I saw Rodney was at a Comedy Central awards show in 2003, a year before he died. He had just had brain surgery and looked very frail. I had not seen him in at least ten years, but he saw me and smiled and said, "Hey, Essie!" Then he looked over his right shoulder and said, "What are you doing?" which was in reference to a bit of mine he always liked. In the bit, I talk about running into an old boyfriend and not being able to remember anything about the relationship except every night in bed saying, "What are you doing?" as I look over my shoulder, behind me. You kind of need the visual, so I'm sure this isn't translating, but the point is, Rodney remembered the joke. He always remembered a good joke. He had a great comedic brain.

Comedians are a unique breed. We see the world through a skewed lens. We're outsiders sharing our oblique image of the world. An abstract painter can look at a woman and see all sorts of shapes. The comedian looks at the same woman and sees something funny about the way she looks or her turn of phrase or attitude or her body language. Both are seeing something that others don't notice, and both need to express that something.

The cliché that comedians are unhappy, damaged people is only partially true. I know a lot of unhappy, damaged comedians. I also know a lot of happy, damaged comedians. I think comedians may seem more unhappy because they are unable to screen out the negatives of life as effectively, and because of the way our brains work, we speak our thoughts, and humor becomes a way to cope with seeing reality too clearly. Rather than deny the injustices and ironies of life, we make fun of them. Comedy is about paying attention.

There's something about making people laugh. It's actually not that hard to do once you figure a few things out. Any schmuck with a bit of timing and lack of self-consciousness can get up onstage and put a hot dog up his nose, or tell fart jokes with energy and charisma and get an audience to laugh. Hacky, mediocre comics make audiences laugh with generic, predictable material all the time. The audience doesn't seem to mind. They often don't know. There is a base level that gets us all giggling. Comedy is very primal in many ways. It thumbs its nose at the polite and appropriate. And that's a good thing. I'm not a snob about comedy. People want to laugh and be entertained, and that's the comic's job.

But there are levels of comedy to strive for that are more difficult to achieve and therefore much rarer. Comedy that uses language and rhythm and nuance to say things never said before, new things, new ideas . . . Comedy that makes people think and feel *and,* at the same time, makes them laugh.

And then there's "the need." The need to be onstage has to be enormous or else none of us would ever do it. It's sort of like a nun answering a calling to God, a pre-op transsexual going through with the surgery . . . doing it is not a question; it's a given. I've always thought that stand-up was a healthy response to a neurotic need.

When I was a kid, maybe five or six, I used to have a fantasy that there was a sitcom about me on Mars. The cameras followed me all the time, and they were always watching. The Martians thought that I was the cutest little Earthling they'd ever seen. I wasn't psychotic and knew that it wasn't really true, but it was comforting. Whether real or not, I felt seen and heard and loved and adored, and it got me through the day. That's a poignant memory for me. It makes me sad for my little self but also marvel at my ability to use my imagination to give myself what I needed. When I was even younger, I had an imaginary friend named Bonnie. I named her after a girl who had been mean to me in nursery school. I was trying to fix the damage. Turn it around. I was going to make her be nice to me even if it wasn't reality. I was always trying to fix reality. Stand-up was the ultimate fix. And you know what? It worked. Between the stand-up and my ten years of psychoanalysis, which, not coincidentally, coincided (and I don't know if I could have survived the early years of stand-up without it), I fixed a lot of things. As corny as it sounds, by healing others with laughter, I was slowly healing myself.

In the beginning—and "the beginning" lasted a long time—I perceived my relationship with the audience as an adversarial one. I lusted for power and glory, and stand-up can indeed provide both. It's very powerful to stand up onstage all alone and control an audience with just your words and a sound-enhancing phallus. But if I needed the audience to give me power, then they had the ability to take that power away. Deriving my sense of myself from the reactions of frequently drunk strangers was a tenuous existence, to say the least. When stand-up was my life force, it was like a drug. When I did six or seven shows a night, I never got tired—feeding on their love, drunk with power, rushing on that adrenaline high like a junkie needing her next fix.

In those days, there were times when I hated what I did. I felt vulgar and desperate, like the court jester desperately trying to make them laugh to save my life, the geisha girl giving clients what they needed. I sometimes experienced the audience as vampires wanting to suck the blood out of me. There were so many times that I wanted to quit and realized that I couldn't because I was addicted. I needed an audience.

Then there were the other times when my experience with the audience was a glorious thing and they gave me something I never could have given myself. Maybe it was maturity or experience or therapy or gin, but somewhere along the way, stand-up changed for me. As I've said before, it takes a long, long time to figure out who you are onstage. I was figuring out who I was in life at the same time. There was no differentiation. Ten, maybe twelve years into it, I started to give up needing the audience to love me and began instead to need them to let me love them. Not a conscious change, but looking back, I can see it rather clearly. I became very free onstage and started to work more spontaneously. Confident and experienced, I rarely went onstage without going into what athletes call "the zone," every show being a peak experience. The audience members were no longer my adversaries; they were my partners.

Ultimately, audiences want to be taken care of—not like a sailor during Fleet Week, but like a passenger on a plane, trusting that the pilot will get them home safely. Yes, they want to laugh; but more than that, they want what we all want all the time—to feel safe and secure. A good comic makes the audience feel safe. You know that unbearably uncomfortable feeling you get when you sit in the audience and watch a bad comic? If you've ever been in a club and seen a bad comic live, you know exactly what I'm talking about. That awkward feeling happens because the bad comic now wants you, the audience, to take care of him. He needs something from you beyond your expectations. That's not why you came to a comedy club in the first place, and if you've had a bad day or are in a bad mood, you may even feel hostility toward the needy comic, who is asking you for something you're not prepared to give. The comic broke the unspoken contract. You, the audience, are there to be entertained and when a comic who is in control, and who knows what she's doing, comes onstage, you can relax and take a passive role, which is what you paid a cover and two-drink minimum for.

From the second I walk on that stage, it's my job as a comic to take control. It's not always easy. Audience chemistry is a strange and unpredictable thing. Audiences, just like comics, have their own personas. There are such things as good audiences and bad audiences. It's interesting how a collection of disparate strangers all take on one collective personality for a finite period of time. I can never figure it out. There are forces out there in the darkness of the theater, energies that I can feel. I'm all alone on the stage having an intensely intimate experience with total strangers. I take in all the needs and fantasy projections—both positive and negative—from the audience. In a split second (a nanosecond if I'm having a really good night), I filter through them. I have them now and I can take them anywhere I want, but suddenly there is a perceptible shift. Something happened. I rapidly go through the file in my head and try to figure out a way to save my ass up there. I furiously comb through the computer chip in my brain, while at the same time I am completely present and in the moment.

They can never see me work. That's the key. That's how I take care of them. I work through the momentary glitch and I'm in the zone again, and some higher power, which I'm not even sure exists, and clearly has nothing better to do, is sending me lines. This thing that's going on between us, performer and audience, is happening in real time. It's never happened before and can never be reproduced, and we are all experiencing it together. I'm leading you, but I never could have gotten here without you. We are in harmony in this moment of perfection that can never be captured or repeated.

Sometimes someone will come up to me in the street and

say something like, "You won't remember me, but I saw you ten years ago at Caroline's Comedy Club and I was sitting in the front and you were talking to me from the stage. I'm Ernie the plumber from Yonkers and I was with my fiancée, Irene," etc. But I DO remember you, Ernie . . . and what's more, I need my drain snaked. What do you charge? It's happened so many times. I remember Ernie, even though I've done thousands of shows in between, I remember because it was experienced so intensely in the moment that it became a part of who we both are. It's the possibility of creation that makes sex so intimate, and I think that applies to audiences as well. We did it together, Ernie the plumber from Yonkers and me, and we were both willing participants, and it was as good for me as it was for you. And yes, Ernie, if it makes you feel good, you were the best—now just leave your money on the dresser, and tippy-toe out, like all the others.

In some ways, doing stand-up hasn't gotten any easier all these twenty-five years later. I still suffer from stage fright. I never know if the muse is going to leave me, go to the ladies' room at the wrong time. I'm scared to death. And now that I draw my own crowds, which in a different way is an absolute pleasure, they expect something from me, and I don't want to disappoint them.

The minute I step on the stage I'm fine, relaxed and in control, but before I go on, I put myself through hell. Don't even ask what I put my husband through! My anxiety level in the hours before I perform is so high that I find it necessary to tell Jimmy everything wrong with him. And whatever he says to appease me and calm me down is wrong.

"Honey, you'll be fine. You always do great. When was the last time you didn't do well?"

I hate when he says stuff like that!

"This time! This is the time when it's all going to disappear!"

"They're going to love you. They're all here to see you."

"That's the problem. They expect me to be funny! There's no funniness in my body right now! I don't feel funny. I have nothing to say to these people."

"Yes, you do. You've got that new bit you've been working on."

"Yeah, WELL I'M NOT GOING TO REMEMBER IT! I'm going to go blank."

"I'll leave you alone so you can focus."

"Where are you going? You're going to leave me here ALL ALONE?"

I drive him fucking crazy, but by now he knows how to ignore me and not take it personally. He knows that I go into a state of pre-show mental illness and that once I come off, I'll be my sweet, loving self again. Last year, a few days before I was scheduled to headline at Caroline's Comedy Club in New York, Jimmy said to me, "You know what I'm really looking forward to?"

"What?" I asked.

"The cab ride down to Caroline's," he said.

I married the right guy.

When the anxiety gets really bad (and sometimes it's unbearable), I call Joy. She's the only one who really understands what I'm feeling—the depth of the fear and why I have to go onstage anyway.

135

It's no fun going through that pre-show torture, but I don't know how to not do it to myself and I'm afraid—superstitiously, I suppose—that if I don't do it, then I really might bomb. I guess I'm stuck with it, because I plan on doing stand-up for the rest of my life. I don't know what else I could do that would be as gratifying as making people laugh. I don't know what else I could do that would fill that empty hole of need so well. Nobody gets hurt and everyone goes home happy and I get paid and feel loved and needed and my husband still loves me in spite of how crazy I am, and in the end, I don't really have a choice. Nobody does this unless they absolutely have to.

CHAPTER 10

THE BRIDE IS KEEPING HER NAME

Susie Essman
Jim Harder

Susie Essman, a comedian and a star of "Curb Your Enthusiasm," was married Saturday to Jim Harder, a commercial real estate broker, at the Friars Club in Manhattan...

The bride, 53, is keeping her name. The couple met in New York during Thanksgiving weekend of 2003. "He was a person who was warm and loving and real," she said in a tender voice that would never have come out of the mouth of Susie Greene, the husband-bashing character she plays on HBO. "He didn't know who I was or that I was on this hit show...and maybe that was a good thing because if he had ever seen me play Susie Greene, he probably would have run for the hills."

Mr. Harder said: "I just kept noticing her. People had told me that she was the funniest person they had ever met, but when I met her, there was a loving and warm side of her that came across almost instantly."

In December, Mr. Harder took his four children — a boy and three girls ages 10 to 15 — to Central Park, where they ice-skated and met Ms. Essman for the first time.

"It's funny," she added, "I never had any interest in getting married or having kids. I was always having fun and enjoying myself and now here I am, in the middle of this big, wonderful family, and my whole life has turned around."

I recently got married for the first time. And I emphasize *first* time not because I don't think it will last but as far as first marriages go, I'm relatively old. Not old old: paleontologists aren't calling me for phone sex. I don't get *Wish you were here* cards from the Leakeys. But old compared to when people usually get married (especially for the first time). Most women my age are working their way through their second or third spouses. I easily could have been one of them. If I had married any of the men I was involved with in the past, then I would have been a multiple divorcee. And much as I like the chicness of the word *divorcee,* I don't know that I would have wanted to actually be one.

I've always known that Jimmy was Mr. Right, as opposed to Mr. Right Now, or Mr. Right Away. From the very early stages of our relationship I felt committed to him and confident that we were going to spend the rest of our lives together, yet I didn't really see the point in getting married. I didn't feel the need to be sanctioned by the church or the state or the caterers, and I wasn't going to have kids because Jimmy already had four and I think that's plenty. Besides, I already had all the appliances I could ever want and have luckily reached the point in my life where I could actually spend my own money on housewares (there were many lean years of hand-me-downs).

Truth be told, I was cynical about marriage. I never saw a lot of marriages that I envied. I work in show business, an industry not known for its relationship with relationships; a field where long-term wedded bliss is the exception, not the rule. For every Tom and Rita Hanks, there is a slew of Elizabeth Taylor Hilton Wilding Todd Fisher Burton Burton Warner Fortenskys.

Additionally, the marriages I saw outside show business weren't much better—they might have even been worse, because they lasted longer. Half my married friends told me they never had sex anymore, and half of *them* seemed happy about it. They had replaced intimacy with the comfort and security of familiarity. Some didn't seem to like each other anymore but lived in oxymoronic fear of losing each other. I didn't want that. I feared ending up in some cloying, sexless dependence, layered with resentment.

I wanted something different. I wanted a mature and secure relationship where we could be together but remain separate. I thought we'd be like Jean-Paul Sartre and Simone de Beauvoir. J.P. and Simone lived in the same building but on different floors and never got married but were together for years. The only thing that came between them (other than floors five through seven) was the existential choice between being and nothingness. Cool, if not ideal—the truth is, he blatantly and compulsively cheated on her, not part of my formula for a happy marriage, but then again, I'm not French. The French are so casual about those things. Pas moi.

It took me a long time to find the man I was willing to commit myself to (even the word *commit* is troublesome; one is committed to a mental institution), and I didn't want to ruin it. Jimmy and I were perfectly happy, so why fix what wasn't broken? Why, after five years of unwedded bliss, did we decide to get married? I'm not really sure. We didn't have to for any reasons—physiological, psychological, financial, or familial. It just came to a point where we wanted to. Jimmy asked and I said yes. Well, he didn't exactly ask. We took a ride to Columbia County, the bucolic county next to our suburban one, where we were going to stop at a quaint little inn for lunch. Sounds romantic, but somehow (we both were in need of a bathroom and starving and a little lost) we ended up at a diner in the middle of a run-down town that was three degrees removed from a trailer park. We were the only people there with teeth. I'm not sure if Jimmy had a marital master plan or if he was, in that moment, simply dazzled by the fact that I had a full complement of cuspids and molars, but all of a sudden he said, "I've been thinking about it and I think we should get married." To which I lovingly replied, "That's not in the form of a question." I felt just like Alex Trebek. He was about to rephrase it as a question when my phone rang. Now, I don't usually answer my phone when I'm in the middle of being proposed to, but I saw that the call was from Julianna, his (and now our) seventeen-year-old, and I felt I should answer, because she had called a few minutes earlier very lost on her way to pick up her sister from the train station and in need of directions. I had a vision of fifteen-year-old Cyndi stranded at the station with Julianna, going endlessly around some traffic circle. It was worse. Her car had broken down in the middle of the highway and she and Cyndi were stranded and hysterical. Having watched every episode of *Law & Order* and *Homicide: Life On The Streets,* I knew a crisis when I saw one, and I told

Jimmy we had to leave immediately to rescue them. Jimmy, who clearly didn't pay attention to scripted one-hour dramas, said he wanted to finish his omelet. We compromised and he got it to go. We got there, waited in the scorching heat for the tow truck, then took Julianna and Cyndi to lunch, because after all, only Jimmy had eaten. When we got home, we were going to take a walk and pick up where we'd left off, but Cyndi, his (and now our) fifteen-year-old wanted help activating her new cell phone and I had promised her I'd take care of it. A scant three hours later Julianna needed help with an essay for her college applications and I had also promised to give her a hand. Sounds both dramatic and mundane at the same time, right? *This* is what I would be marrying—a guy with four kids (teenagers!) who lived with us and whose needs were as endless as teens' needs inevitably are.

Well, what the hell? I had taken on the responsibility for them anyway whether I was legally their stepmother or not, so that wasn't a deciding factor. So, why not? Why not marry the guy? I loved him, I loved his kids, I'd never been married, and I was sure he was the right one. Why not take the plunge and experience something new? It would be an adventure! When the day was finally over, I crawled into bed and said to Jimmy, "Was there something you wanted to ask me?"

Two weeks later we had a wedding.*

People keep asking me if marriage feels different. Yes, it does. I don't know how to explain it. I feel safer. It shouldn't make a difference, but it does. One of the things Jimmy said

---

* (See chapter 11 for how to plan your wedding in seventy-two hours.)

in his wedding vows was that he would "protect me from the villains." (He then invaded the wrong country, looking for weapons of mass destruction, but that's a whole other story.) I feel more secure as a married woman. I didn't expect to feel this way. I guess it's the ball-and-chain thing, but in a good way. There's a tremendous advantage to getting hitched when you're older. First of all, I'd already slept with everyone I'd wanted to except for Pat Buchanan, but he never gave me the time of day. And second, I don't even remember the men with whom I've slept anymore. Sometimes I run into a guy from my college days or from my twenties, and I have some vague sense that I might have had some kind of sexual contact with him, but I'm not sure. I've got to rack my brain, and then I give up because I really don't care one way or another. I'm over it. Now wild oats are something I eat to lower my cholesterol. I was finally ready to settle down with no regrets. I wasn't going to look at Jimmy five or ten years from now and think about my lost youth. I was too old for that. I've seen those couples who've been together for sixty years and look at one another one day when they're eighty and think, "I can't believe I spent an entire lifetime with this asshole." I have no fear of that happening. Worst-case scenario, I'll have spent half a lifetime.

Saying "my husband" still sounds so odd to me and gets stuck in my throat. I kind of like saying "my boyfriend" better. I don't think I'm in danger of becoming one of those women who refer to their spouse as *"my husband"* in bold italics so that you know the man is theirs; he belongs to them . . . just like an iPhone or a bathrobe. But one must remain vigilant. In my wedding vows I did say, "I promise to always be your wife but to always be your girlfriend too." *Girlfriend* sounds so much more fun, and I don't want to give that up.

I couldn't have done this ten or twenty years ago. I was too restless—too curious and fearful. I always thought if wedding vows went something like "For better or worse, richer or poorer, in sickness and in health and you'll never have sex with anyone else for the rest of your life," people wouldn't be so quick to say, "I do." Besides, I don't think it's natural, especially if you're young. So you marry a guy when you're twenty-five and that's it? That's the extent of your sexual experience? That wasn't for me. I probably would have ended up cheating on him or he me and it would've gotten ugly. I don't think most young people think it through before they make the decision to marry.

Think about it. Imagine you marry a guy named Stewie and stay together for fifty years. Every morning you wake up and there's Stewie. Every night you go to sleep and there's Stewie. Stewie in the morning, Stewie at night. Stewie in the morning, Stewie at night. Put a gun to my head! And Stewie, whoever you are, it's nothing personal. It's just too much Stewiness. Don't you think that one day you're going to want a Tom, Dick, or Ira?

But I digress. The whole reason I began to write about the wedding and the marriage was to bring up the issue of—**The Wedding Announcement!**

Putting the wedding announcement in the *New York Times* was one of the biggest decisions I had to make during the whole wedding planning process, not because I didn't want it in there but because I was told that if they put the announcement in, they'd have to include my age. It was quite a dilemma (and you thought Sophie had to make a tough choice!).

Now, I happen to look good for my age. I don't say this boastfully, just honestly. Every now and again I run into some of the women I went to high school with and they look positively ancient (which, I must say, thrills me to no end). In fact, I know women younger than I am who look like they're twenty minutes away from having an attendant give them a sponge bath. Looking good for my age is not something I take credit for, although I do eat well, exercise, stay out of the sun, and don't smoke. Mostly, it's genetic. Luck of the draw. I have very oily skin and had to suffer though a pimply adolescence, but I'm reaping the benefits now. My father, even when he was sick and dying, always looked ten years younger than he was. (Thanks for the DNA, Dad.)

So if I look good, then what's so bad about revealing my age? "It's bad for business" was the excuse I always gave myself. I work in a very ageist industry. If I'm a fifty-year-old woman who can easily play forty, the powers that be, who know that I'm fifty, still won't cast me as a forty-year-old. And I'll never get cast as a fifty-year-old woman because there are very few roles for fifty-year-old women, and the ones that do come along are always played by Meryl Streep, Glenn Close, or Harvey Fierstein.

Hollywood is tremendously youth oriented. Those little girls in their tiny little black dresses have it rough. There's always someone prettier and younger and thinner around the corner. The minute they see a wrinkle they begin doing disfiguring things to their faces. There's an entire group of women of a certain age in Hollywood who look exactly alike. They are all way too thin and have enormous heads and the same face. It's scary. I get all confused when I meet one of them and think I've met them before. It's a catlike thing happening, with the pulled-back eyes, and cheek implants, and eerily smooth buffed skin, and oh, the plumped-up lips! Someone tell them to stop it with the lips. It's horrible. Their lips are beginning to outweigh the rest of their body and make them look like aliens or freaks. It's all so wrong. Do these women actually look in the mirror and think that anyone thinks that's natural? You know how you see a guy with a rug on his head and think, *Didn't he look in the mirror before he left the house? Can he really think that looks good and that no one knows?* That's how I feel about the puffed-up lips. I don't want to mention any names, but there are certain actresses in Hollywood—talented actresses who have more going for them than just a pretty face—who have destroyed their perfectly good looks with collagen lip implants. Like the man in the rug, they look desperate and sad. And no one is going to be calling them when full-lipped Angelina turns the part down. Luckily, I always assumed that I'd be more castable as I got older. I'm a character actress and a comedian—not some pretty little ingénue. I figured I'd grow into those Lainie Kazan roles or, even better, the Thelma Ritter roles, so why not tell my age? Business, schmisness . . . it's vanity pure and simple.

Since the whole wedding, marriage, and Mr. & Mrs. decision happened so quickly and I didn't have a lot of time to think about it, I made the choice to put an announcement in the *Times* in spite of revealing the well-kept, or maybe not so well-kept, secret of my age. Besides, the wedding was a last-minute thing, so I thought the announcement in the *Times* was more expedient than sending out my own wedding announcements. You'd be surprised how many people read that section! Even hetero guys read it! (Okay, not superhetero guys. Not Daniel Craig.) The announcement in the *Times* was great. It really captured us as a couple and told a sweet and loving story about our relationship, and I couldn't be more pleased except for the line that read, "The bride, 53, is keeping her name." 53. Or as it appeared to me, **53**! Now, why was that relevant to the story? Why didn't it say, "The bride, who is gluten intolerant," or "The bride, who got a 1210 on her SATs"? Unless one party is a minor or there's a huge disparity in their ages, like Anna Nicole Smith and the vegetable, I don't see how the age of the bride or groom matters.

I know the *New York Times*'s motto is "All the News that's Fit to Print," but I didn't think that was fit to print! And I certainly didn't think it was news! If the *Times* didn't print the names on Dick Cheney's energy council, my age certainly doesn't qualify as a headline. Yet, there it was, and since the *New York Times* is "the paper of record," the story was picked up by *People* magazine, *Entertainment Weekly*, and several other publications, and every one of them, when describing me, said, "Essman, 53 . . ." There, big as life, jumping off the page . . . ESSMAN, 53 . . . ESSMAN, 53 . . . Why didn't they just write, "Essman, dowager crone"? But as stunning as it looked in print to me, turns out most people didn't even notice it. Which was a little upsetting in and of itself, because it implied that they assumed I was 53 and not surprised by it. Thankfully, there were a few kindly folks who did say they always thought I was much younger. Phew!

After a while, a strange thing started happening to me. I began to feel liberated by the disclosure. My dirty little secret was out, and I didn't care who knew it. In fact, I couldn't stop telling people my age. I'd tell anyone . . . agents, managers, the homeless . . . I couldn't wait to say it. "Hi, I'm fifty-three years old." It became a big *fuck you.* A dare, almost. "Stop me if you can, but I'm going to tell you whether you like it or not." It was borderline Tourette's-ish.

Since I'm in full disclosure mode, I hereby confess that about five years ago, I did Botox once and Restylane three or four times and it looked good. I saw the difference. But it gave me the creeps. I could feel the liquid going into my body and I didn't like it. Twice, I got sick a few days after I got the injections. The first time was mild and could have been from any number of things, but the second time, a week after a Restylane injection, I got very sick with a high fever that went up to 106. Now, there was not necessarily a cause and effect, but there was in my mind, and I haven't done it since. I will never again inject a foreign substance (besides Jimmy) into my body.

And I doubt I'll ever get cosmetic surgery either. Elective surgery seems nuts to me. So much can go wrong. The doctor could sneeze while doing my chin and for the rest of my life I'll be having a bad face day! Why test fate? But what if I didn't look good for my age? What if I looked like shit? Would I do the injectibles and the surgery? I don't know. You'll have to check back with me in ten years. Vanity sure is powerful, and I guess it depends on whether or not I'm working.

The only nonnatural concession to vanity I'll make is that I will continue to color my hair—and I'm not so sure if that's vanity or just good business. There are not a lot of silver-haired actresses in Hollywood. Go ahead, name thirty. Okay, name five!

It's different for men. Cary Grant looked good with silver hair, and Lee Marvin did too, but you know what? They're both dead. I'm not saying they'd be alive if they used Just For Men, but you never know. Maybe one day, when I'm retired, I'll let it go and become one of these crazy old frizzy-haired women I see on the Upper West Side of Manhattan yelling at kids to stop cursing, pick up their litter and recycle, and learn to respect their environment! Wait a minute, I'm already that woman.

I've become that old lady and I like her. I get into fights on a daily basis. I'm the self-appointed rudeness police, and I'm horrified by the pervasive lack of manners and decorum today. Recently, I was in a small convenience store and a bunch of high school boys came in to buy something. One of them lit up a cigarette. I politely asked him to put it out (we were in very close quarters) and he got all mouthy with me, trying to show off in front of his friends. I very calmly said to him, "Listen, kid, I'm going to do you a favor and tell you something. When you act rude and cocky like that, women assume that you've got either a really small or really inadequate penis." Then I walked out. He and his friends were speechless. A younger woman could never have gotten away with that. But a fifty-three-year-old woman? Make my day!

Aging is inevitable. It happens to the best of us. Everything hurts and I can feel the cartilage wearing away on my joints, but there's nothing I can do to make the years not go by. I see a certain crepe-paper quality to my skin. It hangs looser on my bones, on my hands and ankles. I think I know what a brisket must feel like. I'm kind of fascinated by it and smile when I look at the veins in my hands popping out. Wow, I'm that person now. That old-skinned person. I remember my grandmother's skin after she moved to Florida. She had an olive complexion, and her skin became extremely tan and leathery, like an animal hide. Her legs were brown and shiny, like a crisp turkey, and there was a sheen to her skin in all its spotted, lizardlike glory. I thought it was so cool. And slowly, I see it happening to me. I'm like some weird science experiment, slowly morphing back into my reptilian self from whence I came billions of years ago. I figure in another couple of years I'll be getting cast on *CSI* as a cadaver. Oh well, work is work.

Once you hit fifty, you're on the downhill slide. The deterioration begins, and, in spite of advertising claims, it's not reversible. The best you can do is maintain. But the maintenance is all consuming. Between my roots and my skin care regime and exercise and the doctor's appointments and let's not forget flossing, there's no time to think about how old I am! I say, embrace it. What the hell, you might as well. That's not to say that we should no longer care about our looks. No, no, no. I love it when I see an older woman on the streets of New York who made the effort to put herself together, even if her coral-colored lipstick *is* up to her nostrils. At least she tried. I'll always do my best to look good, but looking good doesn't mean looking young. Therein lies the mistake. I was in France last summer and saw these fabulous, well-dressed, older French women riding their bikes through the streets of Paris, and I didn't see one case of collagen lips or Botoxed brows. They looked vital and beautiful. On the Riviera all these old broads are on the beach topless with their boobs hanging down to their knees and they're having a grand old time. Let's take a page out of their book—not the topless part, that's a bit much for me—but the comfort-with-their-aging-selves part. Have you seen Brigitte Bardot lately? She looks like a shar-pei. I don't know if that was a motivating factor in her becoming an animal activist or just a lovely irony, but re-gardless, Madame Bardot doesn't care. In fact, in every photo of her taken these days, her eyes seem to be saying, "I'm sixty, I'm wrinkled, and if you don't like it, then fuckez-vous!"

They say that youth is wasted on the young. Bullshit. Age is wasted on the old if all they do is pine to be young. I see my teenage stepdaughters and their obsession with their looks. They're self-conscious about everything. They happen to be gorgeous, and I say that relatively objectively because they're not my biological offspring. Still, they are focused on their looks beyond any necessity and reason. I remember being like that and can see now what a complete waste of time it is. Think back—it wasn't all that much fun. I'm having a way bet-ter time now. If I focus on looking younger as I get older, then the only outcome I can have is misery. Let the young look young. They're supposed to. And while I'll have to say good-bye to certain perks of youthful attraction, like men looking at me in the street (although thank God for black men, who are always there to appreciate women no matter how old or big an ass), I think I'll survive without it. Besides, have you ever stopped to talk to any of those men who make comments to you in the street? Of course not!

If you can accept the aches and pains and wrinkles and creases and dimples, there are many great things about growing old, from the liberation of not giving a shit what people think of you to the freedom of uninhibited sex. Yup, my little ones, sex gets way better as you get older. Especially for women.

So the bride, 53, plans on keeping her name and her crow's-feet and her thinning lips and her middle-aged spread and her spider veins and her self-respect and her ability to really throw it down in the bedroom.

Eat your hearts out, you sweet young things.

CHAPTER
11

YOU'RE IN—
YOU'RE OUT—
YOU'RE MARRIED!

My wedding day,
September 13, 2008

The decision to get married is much easier than actually getting married. Making that decision is kind of simple. You either want to marry him or you don't, and if you're not sure, that counts as a don't. It's making the wedding that will kill you. I can't tell you how many people have told me that if they had to do it over again, they would have eloped rather than have a big elaborate function. Planning a wedding is arduous, exhausting, and stressful—sort of like childbirth with cake—and people often take years to do it. I never got that. It's a party, for God's sake! I was not going to have any of that. I had no interest in spending so much time planning my wedding that by the time I was finished they'd have to carry me down the aisle on a gurney. Not that I was going to walk down the aisle in the first place. There was something that always bothered me about the father walking the bride down the aisle. Not only is there an icky underlying Electra thing going on but the origin of the ritual is that the bride is property, being passed from father to husband, like chattel or a goat or a chicken.

At first Jimmy and I talked about getting married at city hall, but he wanted his four kids to be a part of the actual ceremony, not bystanders, which was not only a beautiful sentiment but also a proper one. After all, I was marrying all of them and they me. I got Jimmy and four great kids, and they got me and a territorial Shih Tzu.

Since I wasn't pregnant, I can't say our wedding was shot-gun, but it *was* put together as quick as a pistol. I actually planned the entire wedding . . . in three days! No overly of-ficious wedding planners, with their pretentious red-framed eyeglasses and BlackBerry microphones clipped to their la-pels, running around barking orders, making everyone crazy. I did it by myself, in seventy-two hours, and it was perfect. So to you women out there who have been planning your big day since the Clinton administration—you are making a huge mistake and wasting valuable time. Time better used for more pleasurable things . . . like shopping or sex, or shopping and sex.

Here's how to put together a fabulous wedding in seventy-two hours:

FIND THE RIGHT PERSON TO PERFORM THE CEREMONY

The importance of getting the right person to administer the vows cannot be overestimated. He or she needs to have the right combination of gravitas and cheer, and must understand both the importance of the occasion and the importance of not turning the wedding into a funeral. Since I don't know any rabbis and Jimmy doesn't know the pope, and since neither of us is particularly religious and it would seem hypocritical to get married under the auspices of a religious institution, and since we didn't want a stranger performing our cere-mony, and since I've met the mayor but we're certainly not friends, I called my good friend, the writer-producer Tom Fontana, who is also a minister of the American Fellowship

Church. He got ordained online, for the sole purpose of performing marriage ceremonies for his friends. He insists that it's legal. Being the good friend that he is, I felt no need to check his credentials and trusted that he wasn't ordained on craigslist. I am forever grateful to the internet and for Al Gore. Marrying us was no easy task for Tom; he had to walk the fine line of pleasing the Catholics (not easy) and the Jews (even less easy). He had to be respectful but not alienating to either side. My Jewish mother would be turned off by too much religion, and Jimmy's Catholic mother would be turned off by too little. I knew that Tom was the perfect choice and I knew he would say and do just the right thing. He created and wrote the HBO series *Oz,* which is about life in a prison. Who better to talk about marriage?

Once we found out Tom's availability, we set the date. It was eleven days away. Let the fun begin. I had to figure out where we were going to have the wedding; what I was going to wear; what we were going to say; what the kids were going to wear; what we were going to eat; get the license, the rings; did we want flowers, a photographer, an announcement in the *New York Times*? I had lists coming out of every orifice in my body.

THE GUEST LIST

You can't figure out the "where" until you figure out the "whom." This is the trickiest part of the whole deal—whom to invite and, more importantly, whom not to invite. I knew we were going to have to be brutal and strict in order for this to work in so little time. We decided to invite only immediate family, but immediate family means different things to different people. To my mother it includes aunts, uncles, cousins, *her* friends, and some woman named Bernice she once met at the dry cleaner's. My mother waited a long time for me to get hitched and was none too happy when I informed her that it was siblings and parents and our children only. Jimmy is one of nine (Catholic, remember?), and all of his brothers and sisters have a million kids. His side alone could fill Madison Square Garden. Besides, my version of immediate family still added up to thirty-five people. I just didn't want a whole big megillah. I snuck in a couple of friends, but only a couple—three, to be exact—and that was to balance out all of Jimmy's siblings. Besides, I'm the girl, so it's really my wedding, not his. Men would be very happy to simply say "I do" and then go home and panel the den. The bride always rules. Joy Behar is like a sister to me, and everyone knows that there's no way I'd have a wedding and not have her there. Well, since it was such short notice, she had a gig that she couldn't get out of and she couldn't attend. I thought about changing the date, but it was too complicated. It all worked out beautifully, though, because when other friends asked why they weren't invited, I simply said, "Look, even Joy wasn't there" and that was that. In the end, much as I would have liked her to be there, she did me a big favor by not coming. A little bending of the truth, but it worked like a charm. Oh, and Jeff Garlin, my TV husband, came too. He called the night before the wedding to tell me he was in town and I told him I was getting married the next day. He insisted, as the only husband I'd ever previously had, that he had to be there. It was novel and fun having my two husbands there together. And besides, the kids loved Jeff. He sat at the kids' table and entertained them all afternoon. Who needed a magician?

I told everyone that we'd have a big celebration with our friends at a later date, which has yet to happen . . . and never may because most of my friends have already sent us gifts and besides, I'm exhausted just thinking about the guest list. Choosing a guest list is like the president picking his cabinet; there are a finite number of seats available and lots of qualified candidates to fill them. Where do you draw the line? Who's a friend? An acquaintance? A business associate? In my business, it's hard to tell. The boundaries are fuzzy, if nonexistent. People I barely know have told me their innermost secrets at some industry party. It's like they all think that life is one big group therapy session. But I digress . . . now that I narrowed down the "who" (or is it "whom"?) it was time to deal with the "where."

LOCATION, LOCATION, LOCATION

Jimmy and I were married at the New York Friars Club. It's not exactly St. Patrick's Cathedral or Temple B'nai 'Yshraim, but in the world of comedy, it's a shrine. I'm a Friar and proud to be part of its long legacy of comedians and entertainers. The club is located in a gorgeous old town house in midtown Manhattan, and although the Friars are known more for their roasts than marriages, it seemed an appropriate venue. Jimmy is my soul mate, and the Friars Club shares a piece of my heart. Besides, they were the only ones that would accommodate me on such short notice. Membership really does have its privileges. I'd get married there again anytime . . . to Jimmy of course, when we renew our vows in ten years. Ah! That's when I'll have the party!

All the rooms in the club are named after show biz luminaries . . . Frank Sinatra, Lucille Ball, Ed Sullivan. Our ceremony was held in the George Burns Room. I love the symbolism of getting married in the George Burns Room. George Burns and his wife, Gracie Allen, had a legendarily great marriage. George always let Gracie get the laugh, and he loved it. He was Gracie's straight man, and Jimmy is mine. When George was asked the secret to a successful marriage, he replied, "Marry Gracie." George outlived Gracie by thirty-two years, and to ease the pain of her loss after she died, he used to sleep on her side of the bed. Now that's love and devotion. I thought the choice of room was a good omen. The reception was in the Milton Berle Room. Milton Berle was legendary for something else entirely, which also bodes well for a happy marriage.

WHAT'S A WEDDING WITHOUT FLOWERS?

While flowers do not a wedding make, a wedding without flowers feels like a driver's license renewal at the DMV. I could try to sound poetic and say that flowers symbolize the spring of a new marriage, or they represent the love that is blooming between the bride and groom, but the truth is, flowers look and smell great, and not having them just reeks of cheap.

In our case, finding the perfect florist with perfect taste was easy. Jimmy's brother, Mike, is a wedding florist, among other things, and he did the most beautiful job. He has incredible talent and even better taste. Well, of course he does, he's gay . . . quelle surprise! And even better than the beautiful work he did was the fabulous break on the price he gave us! (It really isn't what, but who, you know . . .) Mike didn't just do the flowers for the wedding; he also planted the seeds for the entire relationship. I met Jimmy through Mike. I don't want to lavish undo praise on him for that, because he didn't mean to set us up. We just happened to end up in the same place at the same time—although it wasn't completely accidental, because Mike's boyfriend put the bee in my bonnet about Jimmy long before I met him. Mike and I had been close friends for about ten years. He'd seen me go through various relationships with various men, yet he had never thought to set me up with his brother. In his words, "Why would I think you'd go for a divorced father of four who lived one-hundred-fifty miles away and didn't have lots of money?" But Mike's boyfriend, Jordan, who is a casting director by trade, thought differently. He thought Jimmy and I would mesh. So he arranged a casual, "Oh look, Jimmy, it's Mike's friend, Susie" kind of a moment one weekend when Jimmy was in town. Although "arranged" is a bit of an exaggeration—Jordan had told me Jimmy was hot and that I'd like him and then he'd told me where they'd be having brunch. Guess who showed up? Needless to say, Jordan is a *very* good casting director. In fact, he's as good at casting—after all, he cast Jimmy as my husband—as Mike is with flowers, and Mike is the very best.

CLICK!!

It's important to have pictures of the wedding . . . you know, as evidence at the trial, later. At first, we thought of not getting a photographer and just asking the guests to bring their own cameras, as we have a few amateur Annie Leibovitzes in the family. But after careful consideration, I decided I'd rather not have a photo album filled with people with red eyes or a thumb blocking their faces, so I hired a professional. And I'm glad I did. It was worth it. Lisa Berg, who has been a photographer for NBC News for years and has photographed everyone from Bill Clinton to B.B. King, did the honors. She handled everything effortlessly and seamlessly and was everywhere at once while being magically nonintrusive. I have looked at those pictures a million times, and there's nothing like documentation. Without the photos, I might have doubts about whether or not it actually happened.

DELEGATION

I'm a wee bit controlling, so delegating responsibility to others isn't easy for me. I think the only choices I didn't meddle with were the flowers (see above), the gluten-free wedding cake that my sister Nina got for us, and the wine that Lorraine Bracco and her brother Sal generously sent from their winery. Part of it was that I don't fully trust anyone to do it exactly the way I want it done, and part of it was that there was so much to do in such a short time that it was easier to just go into obsession mode and get it done. Along with London and Paris, obsession mode is one of my favorite places, a place where my mind is so preoccupied that there's no room for anything else. It's why I love decorating. I love waking up in the middle of the night with my head spinning with ideas. Spin, spin, spin. Total preoccupation. Other than bossing people around, there's nothing I enjoy more than crossing things off my to-do list. Sheer joy. Planning a wedding in such a short time takes total and complete focus. I was also in the middle of shooting a movie, so I really had to compartmentalize. I was so busy that I didn't have time to panic about the fact that I was about to get married. The day before the wedding, I had a long list of errands, and Andy, my soon-to-be stepson, was taking the train to New York from Boston, where he goes to school (another thing that was crossed off my list—buy Andy a train ticket). He called me from the train to tell me he had nothing to wear the next day. He was twenty years old, couldn't he dress himself? That was all I needed the day before the wedding. I ran around to three different stores and bought him a variety of pants, shirts, and sport jackets to try on the next morning: cutting it close, but it kept me occupied and free from worry. I felt like my dog when I take him to the vet's office. We distract him with cookies and he's oblivious to the fact that he's getting shots. While I was cursing him the whole time, down deep I was secretly relieved to be so immersed in minutiae.

Andy totally redeemed himself the next day when he gave a very funny and heartfelt toast at the reception. That was another thing I delegated, or assigned. I asked—or, they might say, told—a number of people to prepare something to say. Toasts make a party and we were, after all, at the Friars Club.

It was great, from my sisters' song parody, to Jimmy's brother ripping him apart in true Friars roast fashion, to everyone in between. We loved it.

THE DRESS

I think that for the bride the only thing more important than picking the right husband is picking the right dress. I didn't have a whole lot of time to shop and I certainly wasn't going to wear a white wedding gown, which is yet another tradition that can be traced back to sexist roots. I'm not a virgin, have no interest in being a virgin, and even less interest in perpetuating the concept that being a virgin when getting married is a good thing. I believe in test-driving a car before I buy it, so no white for me. It was a brunch, so I didn't want anything too dressy, but still, I wanted it to be special.

Time was running out. Even though I wanted something new to wear, I decided to look in my closet just to see what I had, and there it was—my mother's wedding dress, which had been hanging there for years—right between the riding crop and the naughty nursemaid costume. I don't know why I had my mother's wedding dress—or the nursemaid costume, for that matter—hanging in my closet, but I did. Was I unconsciously waiting to wear it? It was, after all, in *my* closet, not in either of my married sisters'. I put it on and it fit perfectly. It was purple velvet and midcalf length. Very 1940s. My mother was clearly ahead of her time and very hip for 1948, which is when she married my father, and I don't think the dress had been worn since. I wore a pair of red patent leather shoes. It was a great combo. My mother cried when she saw me in it—although I don't know if that was from sentiment or if she just couldn't believe she ever fit into a size 6!

WRITE THE VOWS

This was hard for me. I know how to get up in front of people and be funny, but to be serious and personal was difficult. I didn't want it to be too sappy, like a Michael Bublé concert, but I took these vows very seriously. I waited a long time to make them, and I wasn't going to say anything I didn't mean and I wanted to mean everything I said. I whisper sweet nothings to Jimmy all the time, frequently using phrases like "Stop acting like an asshole!" but to say intimate things in front of our families and children made me feel extremely vulnerable. I think I got it almost right. Jimmy's vows were so beautiful and heartfelt, and I cried. All four of the kids read passages and I cried some more, and then the Catholics said an Our Father and Jimmy broke the glass, and the Jews yelled mazel tov and the deed was done, and I cried again. Then we ate, drank, toasted, talked, laughed, and everyone went their separate ways. It was a perfect day and the whole thing was planned in under a week.

ONCE AGAIN, for me, life imitates art. I'm a comic. Set it up, knock it down, and get out. I'm of course referring to the wedding, not the marriage. I'm planning on sticking around in that for a good long while.

163

E verybody is so hysterical about everything. I have two words for those people: calm the fuck down. Okay, four words. But not really, especially if you elide the *the, fuck,* and *down.* Relax, relax, relax, my frantic little friends; whatever it is that you're worrying about is, most likely, out of your control. There are forces at work in the universe that neither you nor I have power over. Yet we fret. If I worry about something, then I think I have some kind of influence over the outcome. Nonsense. I'm just not that omnipotent. It's not all about me, and it's certainly not all about you. Harsh? Perhaps, but assuming you're based in reality, absolutely true. The next time you find yourself worrying that other people are talking about you, conspiring against you, or pondering your magnificence, just remember: you're not that important. No one's thinking about you. No one gives a shit.

A few years ago I was at a wedding and ran into a former club owner I hadn't seen in about ten years. To protect the guilty, let's call him Bob. We'd had a falling out because he had screwed me in some business thing—he screwed a lot of people and was subsequently put out of the business, thus accounting for my not seeing him all those years. He came over to me and said, "I know you hate me." And I responded, "Honestly, Bob, I don't hate you. I don't ever think about you." I wasn't trying to be mean, it was just the truth and came out that way. Well, apparently, according to a mutual friend, this was the most devastating thing I could have said to Bob. He talked about it for weeks. He would have much rather been hated than irrelevant. But why should I even have bothered giving him the kind of energy it takes to hate someone? I didn't care enough about him.

All those years he was worrying about all the people who hated him and nobody gave a crap about him. He wasn't that important. Everyone's thinking about themselves and how to survive. Look, I get the anxiety level, but let it go. It's not helping.

In the not-too-distant future, the earth is going to become a barren, bleak, lifeless wasteland. Okay, so maybe it's a billion or so years away, and even with healthy diets, omega-3 supplements, and exercise, none of us will be here to experience it, but it's still going to happen. Maybe the sun is going to implode or dry up, as I learned from a show on the National Geographic Channel, or maybe we'll all be eaten by wild Dobermans who are staging a mass revolt against Cesar Millan. Perhaps a giant tsunami triggered by an earthquake or volcanic eruption in Indonesia or a hurricane caused by rising sea temperatures will wipe out the entire East Coast of North America. That includes New York, by the way. Right now, as I write this, I'm looking at the Hudson River, waterway/landing strip, and for some delusional reason I think that in case of an actual natural disaster, my lovely two-bedroom apartment with western exposure will somehow be protected because I'm on the tenth floor of my building. How ridiculous! I actually think that I'm safe! Oh, mes amis, the games we play.

Did you know that the universe is expanding? It is. Not quite as fast as the waistlines of American children, but still a little too quickly for my comfort. There are billions and billions of stars and galaxies out there, and they're all moving away from the planet Earth. They are fleeing us like we're a French cathouse during a police raid or something. It's all spinning out of control.

And let us not forget the whole asteroid smashing into the earth thing. It could be heading our way as you read this and it would make a nuclear winter look like a day at the beach. Oh, and there's that too—you know, the "nuclear thing." I mean, don't you think eventually that some mad man or woman is going to pull the trigger on one of these devices? How long can we live like this? It's going to happen, either purposefully or accidentally, so prepare yourselves for one prolonged, intense hot flash. Not that prep makes a difference on this one. Having a first-aid kit, duct tape, and bottled water isn't going to mean squat if it comes down to it.

So our civilization and everything we've accomplished and everything we know will be gone forever. Don't feel so bad, something else will come along and take our place. Okay, it may not be as fabulous as Karl Lagerfeld or a banana split, but something's going to live again. In the larger scheme of things we're just a blip, a speck. Dust bunnies under the sofa of the universe. The earth is 4.6 billion years old, give or take a few hundred million years, and *Homo sapiens*—that's us— or most of us—have been around for 120,000 years. We only diverged from the chimp 5 million years ago and the gorilla 8 million years. Of course none of this is true for you if you believe in the literal interpretation of the Bible, a book written by, as they say in Hollywood, committee. Or should I say, committee of men. I always thought all of our lives would be a whole lot better if the Bible had been written by a woman, but back then, women were barely taught to read and write, so that wasn't going to happen. Can you imagine how much more interesting Leviticus would have been if Danielle Steele or Edith Wharton had had a crack at it? And believe me, Eve would have told that snake to go shove it if the whole thing was written from a woman's point of view. For a piece of really good-quality dark chocolate, maybe—but an apple? Never happen.

According to the testostoterrorists who wrote the Bible, the earth has been around for six thousand years. All those prehistoric creatures like the dinosaurs weren't prehistoric at all; in fact, in the planet's early days, they roamed freely along with mammals, reptiles, and Larry King. They became extinct not because of evolution or natural selection or the asteroid that fell in the Yucatan but due to a housing shortage on Noah's ark. My guess is that given their size, and their vain aversion to wearing life jackets, they probably all drowned. I don't know if Noah had some kind of grudge against dinosaurs, or maybe his wife had a limit as to what she was willing to clean up after, but regardless, it wasn't very nice of him to exclude them and showed a terrible and insensitive discrimination against largeness. It does occur to me though that if that's true, then the cartoon *The Flintstones* was prescient by having Dino living along with Fred and Wilma. Living peacefully, I might add, in spite of Dino's occasional neediness over a trunkful of barbecued ribs. Except that if the earth is only six thousand years old, then the caveman Stone Age thing couldn't have happened, let alone barbecue sauce, so the whole concept really doesn't track.

Hmm . . . what about all the evidence? All the fossils and things? Well, here's a theory I've heard: God put all those dinosaur bones in the ground and geological evidence and ancient cave drawings and tools and Lucy's skeleton, etc., just to test our faith. Apparently, a burning bush and a woman made of salt weren't good enough for him. What a trickster that God is, huh? ("He'll be here all week, folks! Please tip your waitresses.") God put all this evidence out there, right in front of us, that evolution exists, but reality-challenged masses are choosing to ignore it. Instead, they believe in the unsubstantiated claims that a group of fallible humans wrote in a language the masses can't even read.

Should we believe what we see? Of course not, believe what someone *tells* you is the truth. Never trust your own eyes. Galileo did, and look what happened to him! They arrested his ass, tried him, and denounced him as a heretic. He spent the rest of his life under house arrest, all because he looked through a telescope, which didn't exist before he devised it, and saw with his own eyes that the sun couldn't possibly revolve around the Earth! What? How could that be? Man is so important that God created us in his image, so we, therefore, must must must be the center of the universe. If God created other stuff before us, then we're not his favorite anymore. Maybe he likes some other species better than us. Like flies, for example. Flies seemingly serve no purpose other than to screw up picnics, yet here they are, in 2009, circulating about in all their disgusting glory. Maybe they're God's favorites . . .

why else would they be here? Think about it—he even gave them wings, and with that, the gift of flight. They never have to go though airport security, yet do they ever fly any-where meaningful? I think not. Maybe God's just toying with us and keeping us around for a few hundred thousand years and then, when the mood strikes him, has us evolve into something yet again. No, it can't be. We are him. We are in his image. I read it, and besides, how can we possibly go on if we're not godlike ourselves? I know of at least six guys in my gym who are thoroughly convinced they are gods; if you don't believe me, just ask them.

Here's a thought: it's not all about you. Maybe God has other things on her mind. (Notice I said "her"? That's my way of pandering to curry favor with the Birkenstock-wearing folksy earth mother types I dissed in the other chapter.) Maybe you—yes, you, Mr. God-loves-me-all-pro-athlete-won-the-foot-ball-game-because-you-prayed-harder-and-louder-than-the-opponents'-quarterback—are not the first thing she thinks of after her morning coffee.

Oh, the narcissism. It's really hard to take. In 1992, the Catholic Church finally did forgive Galileo. That was good of them. He'd only been dead for 350 years. I like to think that with proper counseling and some mood-stabilizing drugs, he's gotten over his anger by now.

I have a solution to the science-versus-religion conflict that has been raging through our citizenry for hundreds of years. I think that all of those people who want to deny observational science shouldn't be allowed to take part in its triumphs. Nope, you shouldn't be allowed to partake in technology, for example. It's all physics all the time, and you can't believe in some of it and not others and pick and choose what's convenient. You can't deny the big bang and then believe in radio waves. So, for all of you science naysayers, here goes . . . you must immediately, upon reading this:

Give back your computers, flat-screens, iPods, and Black-Berries.

Replace your indoor plumbing with an outhouse.

Say bye-bye to cars . . . as well as planes, trains, and all other transportation devices other than horses or mules.

Put your stove, oven, refrigerator, air conditioner, toaster, waffle iron, and George Foreman (the grill, not the man) in the garbage. And mind you, there won't be any trucks coming by to pick up your trash.

Take really, really good care of yourselves, because if you get sick, there won't be any modern medical care for you. (But prayer will work!)

You want to deny facts, then I say you're denied usage of the spoils of those facts. If you know all the answers, then you stop asking questions, and when you stop asking questions, you don't move forward, which means you eventually move backward and none of these modern conveniences would exist. Half that stuff was invented by homosexuals anyway, and besides, you won't be needing any of that crap soon because the asteroid is on its way. I can't wait. I'll be sitting by my digital clock/calendar/sundial counting the days. Armageddon, you say? Nah, God doesn't care enough about us to purposely wipe us out. She's not thinking about us. She's thinking about herself!

My kids and me,
September 2008

Dear Children,

The other day I was reading Polonius's speech to Laertes, from Hamlet. *Not that I sit around reading Shakespeare (I don't), but I was thinking about this chapter and the wise advice I wanted to convey to you and I realized that Shakespeare had already said everything, and in much better prose than I'm capable of. So I figured I could glean some pearls from Polonius. And as expected, there's some good stuff there, because Shakespeare was no dumdum. For example, "neither a borrower or lender be." How true, especially with boyfriends. Could anyone argue the sagacity of such axioms as "To thine own self be true" or "Give every man thy ear, but few thy voice"? Yeah, yeah, all good, but there's a catch—Polonius was pretty much a meddling, bloviating old fool, so his words of wisdom, however good, were treated as empty platitudes.*

"Do as I say, not as I do" doesn't wash.

Maybe Shakespeare was commenting on the uselessness of giving advice. Maybe advice, by its very nature, is banal. It's clearly more important to teach by example and experience. So if my words are going to be hollow, then why bother saying anything at all? Because I can't help myself and there's stuff I want to tell you. I know you can't learn from my mistakes: you've got to make your own, and I've got to sit by and watch in helpless horror. Such is the way of the world. The most difficult part of parenting for me has been to keep my mouth shut and let you live your own lives and make your own mistakes . . . and though I try, I've frequently been unsuccessful at it.

My greatest hope (other than that Mariano Rivera's arm holds up for another three seasons) is that I'm a good example for you. Observing the world around me is part of my job as a comedian. I like to think that I've garnered some knowledge that may be meaningful. So here are some observations, a better word, I think, than advice—*less presumptuous, which may or may not be useful to you as you navigate this minefield of life.*

PAY ATTENTION!

That's it. That's all of them.

Paying attention is the key to life—happy or otherwise—and I'll tell you why: (You didn't think you were going to get off that easy with just a two-word response from me, did you?) If you pay attention, you get out of your head. If you pay attention, you're usually not depressed because you're too busy noticing what's going on around you. If you pay attention, you're engaged with the world. If you pay attention, you're rarely bored. If you pay attention, your curiosity is piqued. Curiosity will keep you alive. That old curiosity killed the cat thing is bullshit propagated by people who are either threatened by questions or horribly allergic to cats. Stay away from them (the threatened people, not the cats). Questions are a good and necessary thing.

It's especially important to pay attention to your own feelings. You're the only person you can really *know, so you might as well not miss out on the opportunity. Besides, you might just be fabulous (and you are!). We can never completely know anyone else anyway, so pay attention to yourself. The better you know yourself, the more you have to give others. Selfishness gets a bad rap.*

In 1984, when I was just embarking on my stand-up career, I read a great interview in the Village Voice *with the writer James Baldwin. It strongly resonated with me. In it, Baldwin said, "...you have to go the way your blood beats. If you don't live the only life you have, you won't live some other life, you won't live any life at all." Well, that's the whole thing in a nutshell. All you really have to know. But in order to go the way your blood beats and live your life, you have to listen to your beating blood. You've got to know yourself, not what other people think of you or want for you, but yourself.*

That's why you've got to pay attention. And by the way, worrying about other people's opinions of you is a big waste of time. What other people think of you is none of your business, and ultimately, it doesn't matter (unless of course that other person is the governor and you're on death row). People will think whatever they need to think. You can't control their thoughts, so why waste psychic energy on it? Trying to figure out what other people are thinking about you is an exercise in writing fiction. You'll never know. Listen, observe, and see how certain people make you feel and others don't. Believe it.

Gravitate toward people who like themselves. They won't suck the life out of you. They need less from you and therefore can see you more clearly. Surround yourself with people who make you feel good about yourself, and I don't mean ass kissers or sycophants. I mean people you are your best self with. People who like themselves are less self-involved and therefore have more to offer.

Trust those feelings when someone makes you feel icky. I'm not saying that friends can't give you criticism and that you can never be wrong or that you should turn away from a friend because she is having a bad day. You know what I'm talking about. The crazymakers, the parasites, the people who drag you into their chaos, their mishegas, the drama queens and kings. Those people who leave you feeling tired and headachy and in desperate need of a nap every time you're with them. Pay attention. Don't get their ickiness on you. You can't fix them and you can't change their minds about anything. They thrive on that stuff. Best thing to do is disengage.

You're going to have a friend who is in a bad relationship, maybe even an abusive one, and she/he is going to come to you over and over and over again crying and hysterical, and it will be the same problem over and over and over again, and because you're a good friend, you're going to give him/her advice and time and effort, over and over and over again, and then nothing is going to change. You're going to be drained and she's going to go back to him and do the same thing all over again, and you'll be left alone, on the couch, exhausted, with an ice pack and two Advil. And when they do finally break up, it'll be the same with the next boyfriend/girlfriend or next drama. It's frustrating, and worse than that, it's boring! Protect yourself. Life is hard and you need your strength. Stay away from energy sappers and emotional vampires. Not enough time or medication.

And one day each and every one of you is going to get your heart broken. I dread it because you'll be in such pain and I'll be powerless to ease it. Everyone goes through it. It's inevitable unless you never really care about another person, and I don't wish that for you. There will be streets you can't walk down, songs you can't bear to hear, and TV shows that will cause you pain to watch. It's brutal. You'll feel like you're going to die without them, but really, why would you want to be with someone who doesn't want to be with you? Try not to confuse happiness with one particular person.

Feelings are amazing things. They're fluid and in constant motion. And even if you question their validity, you've got to pay attention to them, you've got to feel them, because if you don't they get stuck and show up in all sorts of weird ways with consequences that can be physically and emotionally devastating. As scary and unpleasant as the feeling may be, it's not going to just go away.

Frequently when our hearts are broken, obsession takes over, but obsession is never about what we think it's about. I had a friend who was obsessed with The Price Is Right. *She watched it every day, DVRed it when she couldn't be home, tossed in her sleep thinking about Plinko and if only Roz from Long Beach had picked the two instead of the three, she would have won the car. I guarantee you that her obsession was actually about something else. I mean honestly, how obsessed could she be about the exact cost of a case of canned peas? Obsession is always an avoidance of feeling something else. Ultimately, I think it's sadness that we're all avoiding more than anything. But we can't avoid sadness, it's a part of being alive. The idea of living a painless existence has screwed up so many lives. You've got to have the strength to feel the things that make you feel hopeless and alone. If you feel something, it will change, it will move, it will evolve. I promise you.*

We're all afraid of different things at different times. We feel fear for a reason. The fear response is built into our genes to protect us, to warn us to take action. When a lion is chasing you, don't wonder what psychological damage was done to the lion as a cub—run! There are legitimately frightening people and things out there. I'd love to tell you not to be afraid, but I can't. When you pay attention, and look and see, you'll often see things you'd rather not; things about yourself, things about the world, scary things. Sorry. You can't skip it, but you need to imagine what's beyond fear and move toward it.

Goethe wrote, "Whatever you can do, or dream you can, do it. Boldness has genius, power and magic in it." Be bold. Don't let fear hold you back. Don't be afraid to be big. Don't limit yourselves. You may not always get immediate gratification—as a matter of fact, you rarely will—if the gratification is worthwhile. Be patient. Everything changes. It's inevitable. People who can tolerate change, accept change, and adjust to change are emotionally healthier and happier. Observe happy and content people. They're not always the richest or the smartest or the most famous. Do your research. See what they know, study them, not what they say but what they do. Don't take advice from people who spew out a lot of bad ideas. Look at their lives. Do they like themselves? How do they treat people? How do people treat them?

Pay attention to the little things in life, like quiet moments in front of a roaring fireplace, gentle walks on the beach, the sounds of birds chirping . . . okay, I'm making myself *nauseous. By "little things" I mean kindness. Kindness makes a difference. Everyone deserves to be respected—from the homeless person on the street to your boss to some celebrity you think is all* that. Treat everyone respectfully and listen to people when they speak. Hear them and acknowledge them. Call them by their name. You may learn something about them or yourself. No one is beneath you. Do the right thing. You'll never be sorry for it, even if it's not convenient. There is a ripple effect to kindness that you'll never know or see, but it exists. It cascades through the ether. Smile at the bus driver and thank him when he takes your fare even if he doesn't smile back. Maybe he'll remember it later and not yell at his kid when he gets home, and on and on. There is no downside to kindness; it harms you not a whit.

Evil gets so much more attention than good because it's, well, it's so evil, and often utterly incomprehensible. Yet there is so much more kindness in the world than evil. Everywhere you turn there are signs of fraternity, whereas evil is an aberration. It's not necessary. Nothing good ever comes from abusive behavior. The only true regrets I have in life—besides not buying real estate in Manhattan in the 1980s—are any times I was, knowingly or not, mean or unkind to someone. Abusive behavior makes you dislike yourself, which is why one must also be wary of sadomasochistic personalities. They will either make you the abuser or abuse you. If you feel abused, trust it and get out. If you feel like someone is provoking you to be abusive, trust it and get out. Abusive behavior can be subtle and insidious, and if you're doing it, or allowing it to be done to you, just stop it right now. Walk away. Yes, people can change their behavior, but don't bet on it. Besides, it's their job, not yours, to change themselves.

If you pay attention, you can make a difference in people's lives. The more you know yourself and face and accept your *own dark side and complexities, the more you'll understand the limitations and demons of others. We are all in this together. We're born alone and die alone, and along the way we connect in seemingly random ways as we try to make sense of something unknowable and transcendent. It's the connections that make life meaningful. Cherish them and value them and make those connections wisely.*

Life is confusing. Feelings are ambiguous and mutable. You love him, you hate her, you're happy, you're sad, and everything in between. Being able to hold and tolerate contradictory feelings and ideas in your head is the trick in life. And if you really pay close attention, you'll realize that the answers keep changing. It's really one of the most amazing and fun shows to watch. Savor it. You'll see and experience great things out there, like music and art and nature and baseball and love and friendship and humanity.

I don't know if any of this makes sense to you, and I've got so much more to say. Whether you take my blowhard advice or don't, remember, I'm always here if you need me. I said in my wedding vows to your father when I married him, "I promise to always protect and love and care for your children." I meant that and I know that you know that I know that you know that I did. I promise to always pay attention to you and your feelings and your lives. I hope you do the same for yourselves and each other. And if you don't, I'll kick the living shit out of you.

With love and respect,

Susie

CHAPTER

14

*HUM-DING
(DING-DING)
DINGER*

S ex can be dangerous and, as such, should come with a warning label like medication: may cause dizziness, disorientation, confusion, blurry vision, shortness of breath, and total annihilation of your self-esteem. Sexual need makes us do strange things, like sleep with people we normally wouldn't touch even if they were wearing a hazmat suit. Did you ever run into an ex-boyfriend or girl-friend and think, *Was I in a psychopathic dementia when I was having sex with this man every night and twice on Fridays?* Or the even scarier moment when you remember, *Ugh, I talked baby-talk to this man!*

It happens to the best of us. We're all a bunch of liars where sex is concerned. For example, everybody knows that you can't believe anything a man tells you when he's sexually aroused. They lie. Yup, they lie, lie, lie, and you know what? It's not their fault. They just can't help themselves. And I know for a fact they lie—do you know how many times I've been in bed with a guy and he's said, "Oh, baby, this is the best I've ever had"? Trust me, I'm not that good. And I know I'm not because I don't really give a shit.

I once read a study measuring men's leadership qualities; invariably, the best and most convincing liar became the group leader. This should not be surprising to anyone who follows politics. Lying well is a highly valued commodity in our culture. It's part of a skill set prized by power brokers in almost all fields of endeavor. If the whole basis for the male MO is about spreading their seed and getting it out there as much as possible, then in a way, men who lie in order to have sex are our species' heroes. They're just doing their job for the benefit of us all. If it weren't for their persistence, their need to get women into bed at all costs—regardless of the emotional consequences—none of us would exist.

Men have not cornered the market on fibbing, however. Women are big liars too. Men lie to women *in order* to have sex, and women lie to themselves *after* they have sex. I think something happens to women when we have an orgasm with a man; some hormone is released that makes us want to have the man's baby. It's craziness! We convince ourselves that we love him and believe it in every fiber of our body regardless of who or what the man really is. No matter how big of an asshole he is, the desire persists. And the problem is that once he satisfies you sexually, then he has the power to take it away and deprive you of a life force and it becomes very complicated. It's not a conscious thing. If it were, we'd save ourselves a lot of heartbreak. It's some ancient trigger buried deep in our psyches. What other explanation could there be for completely normal, rational, sane women, myself included, repeatedly making grotesque and horrendous choices in romantic partners? Even when we know deep in our bones that he's the wrong guy, the desire persists. Even when all of our friends and neighbors intervene, still the desire persists. With women, the I-want-to-have-his-baby syndrome creates an idealization of someone who's a mere mortal.

I found the guy with the right combo of love and lust, but it took me a really long time and a lot of sampling. And interestingly, it occurred when my procreative days were waning and my eggs no longer had USDA AAA rating. Was I finally able to think more clearly and not simply be ruled by my libido? Was it wisdom, or was I simply released from the hold my biological urges had imposed on me?

Sex rules. Organisms will become extinct if they find sex uninteresting. If our urge and drive to procreate withers, then so does the species, so we should all hope and pray that we remain as horny as ever and that our base instincts are intact.

But what about love, you cry? *Isn't that what separates us from all those other creatures who just have sex for procreation's sake?* Well, that and cable . . . but who's to say that the sex/love combo is a more highly evolved state? That assumption is human hubris. Maybe we just made up love to perk up our sex lives. I'm a big believer in love, but this isn't a chicken-or-egg argument. Sex came first, and without love the species would continue—maybe without as much meaning, but still, we'd survive—but without sex, we're done for big-time.

Here we are in the twenty-first century, with more information, technology, and science than our cavepeople ancestors ever even dreamed of, yet we're probably far more confused than they ever were. Did they know something we don't? Did a cavewoman know that the guy she was wildly attracted to in his furry outfit with the big club in his hand was not inevitably the man who would grant her everlasting happiness? And did the caveman with the biggest club have the biggest dick, or were they overcompensating even back then?

Cavepeople were neophytes where sex is concerned. Sex

was invented billions of years before humans even existed, so basically none of us know anything. If only amoebas could talk, the tales they'd tell of billions of years of sexual activity would probably shock us. Oh, to have been a paramecium a billion years ago when men weren't men and women weren't women.

We think we are so highly evolved and beyond this animalistic stuff. I'm here to tell you that we're not. Look around. Attraction is primal, and is more about procreation than happiness. Lions mate to reproduce, not to cuddle and listen to Michael Bolton CDs. Our genes want us to be prolific, not necessarily secure and loved and needed and cherished, which is why smart women make ridiculously stupid choices. My past is littered with unbelievably inappropriate partners. I've been through some real humdingers over the years . . . or should I say, humDINGDINGDINGers.

I think back to the "ding ding ding" moments, those bursts of clarity, those bolts of reality, those moments when I was with a guy and he said something and the bell went off and I knew I should get the hell out of there . . . yet, I didn't. Upon reflection, I'm appalled at my own behavior. I stayed with men when the bells were ringing so loudly that Marlee Matlin could have heard them, but I, Susie Essman, comic/ actress/auteur, completely fucking ignored them and stayed the course.

The ding ding ding moment can happen at any time in the relationship, even the very beginning. Like the guy who told me, on our first date, that his inner child is Dame Judy Dench. And sometimes it happens later in the relationship, as it did for me with a man who admitted to me one day that his pet name for his penis was Klaus Barbie Butcher of Lyon. And by the way, the fact that men name their penises in the first place is bizarre and must mean something psychoanalytically—I'm just not sure what, but it's probably akin to athletes speaking of themselves in the third person. It signals a disconnect. I remember a guy I once dated who would say things like, "Bob really likes Susie. Bob wants Susie to get naked." And the weird thing was, his name was Alfredo! DING DING DING!

Then there was this one guy who insisted on wearing a lobster bib when having oral sex. And that's when I was going down on him! DING DING DING DING! There was the freak who every time he went to the bathroom made me applaud and say, "Who made a good boom boom?" Why did I stay? Or how about the guy that mentioned scar tissue every time he whispered sweet nothings in my ear and, as if that wasn't bad enough, when he wanted me to meet his mother, he took me to a crawl space under the house. The worst, though, was this one guy who barked every time we did it doggie style. That's a little excessive, don't you think? A woof woof every now and then can be fun, almost kinky, but aggressive, metered, barking every single time? DING DING DING!

Okay, I'm kidding. None of my exes were that bad— although some came awfully close—but the point I'm trying to make is that the love drug can be lethal. We are all searching for the "in love" chemical high. There is no way of knowing in the beginning of a relationship if your feelings are real. You're chemically altered. Your pheromones rule, so you have to be careful.

Some say that passion and heat last for two years. That's how long it takes to conceive, deliver, nurse, and build unhealthy resentments toward his family while he's busy checking his calendar and planning an exit strategy. That sounds right to me. I can't tell you how many relationships I've had that ended after two years. No matter how hot I am for the guy, after about two years, I bolt out of bed one day and say, "I don't think I want this thing being constantly shoved down my throat." And that's it. Over. Done. Finisimo. For twenty-four months you're into it, you crave it, you need it, and then, after twenty-four months and, let's say, a day, you're gagging. That's not to say that some relationships don't keep the heat. Some do. You see these cute old couples holding hands and actually liking one another, and you can tell by the look in their eyes or the veins in their ankles that they still do it. Of course, it's entirely possible that they don't remember who that person is and they're simply happy to be ambulatory and have someone beside them to break the fall.

I wish I could tell you, especially you younger child-bearing-aged women out there, how to figure out all this love and sex stuff, but I can't. Truth be told, I have no idea. I'm just a human being—a fabulous human being—but a human being nonetheless, which, as I've already established, means I'm a complete beginner in the sexual arena. What I do know, however, is that there are simply certain men you should avoid *at all costs* no matter how attracted you are to them for whatever unknown reason. There should be "ding ding ding" laws. If you can nip it in the bud and heed the warning signs before he's deeply embedded in your psyche, then maybe you can get out before the going gets rough and save yourself a lot of tsuris.

People will usually tell you who they are by what they do, so be willing to listen and watch. Here's a partial, incomplete list of ding ding ding warnings that should make you run for the hills and never look back:

A man who tells you intimate details about his exes early on in the relationship. It's sadistic. Besides, doesn't he know that he's never been with any other woman but you?

A man who is only attracted to ridiculously skinny women. Homo alert. He may not know it, but he's gay. Do us all a favor and tell him so he can stop making his dates feel bad about themselves because they aren't built like boys.

A man who asks you questions about yourself just so he can talk about himself. It's bang-your-head-against-the-wall time. You're not an object of affection, you're an object of reflection. Stay out of the sun, you'll get melanoma.

A man who has to ask his parole officer if he can give you a call. (And fyi, if he does get permission, the call will be collect.)

A man who on your first date asks if you've ever slept with a woman.

A man who gets too close into your personal space. He probably has more boundary issues than Israel and Palestine. He'll end up reading your diary, picking off your plate, using your toothbrush, and wearing your panties.

A man who calls his mother Mommy. This is a bad one. Only thing worse is when he calls you Mommy or if he asks you to call him Mommy.

A man who doesn't like to kiss. Either he has gingivitis, halitosis, or intimacy issues. This is a lose-lose situation.

A man who works the phrase *well hung* into every conversation. Show, don't tell.

A man who after six dates tells you that he sometimes (read: always) likes to dress like a woman but he's not gay. And on your seventh date (you have undoubtedly ignored the ding ding ding moment) his purse falls open, and it's filled with dildos, butt plugs, and cock rings. Of course he's straight. And why, might I ask, do these guys always look like cops?

A depressed man. The kind of guy who, when a news story comes on TV about a fatal bus plunge, gets this wistful, Gee-they're-the-lucky-ones look on his face. You aren't the cause of the depression, and you're not the solution. You can't fix him. You'll end up nauseatingly perky and turn yourself into a cruise director.

An old man with a young trophy wife. We're onto you and your sense of inadequacy. You look ridiculous, and nobody is thinking, "Boy, Morris must be really great in bed to get such a hot young babe." Believe me, Morris is hung like an actuary. And if you're a young woman thinking of going out with an older man, it's not all it's cracked up to be. Yeah, he may have money, but massaging some old guy's prostate is not my idea of foreplay. When I put my head on a man's chest, it's not because I want to check if his pacemaker is working.

A man who is paying alimony to any woman named Bambi, Kitten, or Bubbles. He may be the same man as the old geezer above but not necessarily. Young guys make mistakes too.

A man who litters. I once knew a relationship was over because the guy threw an empty Milk Duds box out of his car window. What was he thinking? Who did he think was going to pick it up?

A man who is rude to waiters.

A man who talks too loudly in public.

A man who smells bad.

A man who doesn't love you.

A man who surreptitiously lets you know how much he spent on the date. Typical ploy to watch out for is when he asks you, "How much tip should I leave on a hundred-and-twenty-dollar check?" How stupid does he think you are? Or how stupid is he that he can't do the simple math?

A man who is cheap. A lack of generosity with money foreshadows a lack of generosity of spirit—in short, a miserly grump.

A man with no sense of humor. He doesn't have to be funny, but he's got to be able to laugh at himself or you're in for an arduous road ahead. You don't necessarily have to have the same sense of humor. Women find humor in the whimsy of Jane Austen. Men tend to like stuff like *The Three Stooges.* Three violent morons poking each others' eyes out? We don't get it and we never will. Just make sure you've got two TV sets.

A man who has kids and actually thinks they're all gifted, even the one who eats worms and has to wear a helmet just to have his morning cereal.

A man who doesn't think women masturbate. He gives himself way too much credit. Even worse? A man who thinks that when women masturbate, they're thinking of him.

A man who wears cowboy boots (unless he's a real cowboy, or hung like a horse).

A man who is overly concerned with his appearance. I don't care for a man with a manicure, a tan, or cosmetic surgery (unless of course he's in the witness protection program). Beware of the fastidious man with carefully placed hair, extensive ornamentation, and lots of "product" on his bathroom shelves. Be particularly wary of the man who wears fur. A man in a mink is a sad vision to behold.

A man who is a racist, sexist, anti-Semitic, homophobe, xenophobe or refers to any particular group as "them." The list is endless, and eventually you'll find yourself on it.

A man who is overly critical of his friends. Guess who's next?

A man who is self-loathing. Guess who's next?

A man who hates his mother. Yup. Guess who's next!

A man who belongs to someone else. If he did it to her, he'll do it to you. It's just a matter of time, and even if he doesn't, you'll always know he's capable of it. He probably won't leave her anyway, and then you'll have him all to yourself on Flag Day but you'll be spending New Year's Eve alone. Why inherit someone else's garbage? Besides, he's just some guy. Go find one of your own and keep the sisterhood intact.

THE BUSINESS
OF COMEDY,
PART THREE—

HOW I LEARNED
TO MAKE THE WORLD
LOVE ME BY TELLING
THEM TO GO FUCK
THEMSELVES

*Me and MY OTHER
HUSBAND, Jeff*

One day in December of 1999, my phone rang. It was Larry David. The call came out of left field; well, not really left field, maybe more like short center field . . . I knew Larry from our stand-up days at Catch A Rising Star, so it's not as though he was calling some strange woman he'd met online. Still, I actually hadn't seen him in many years. To the best of my memory, this was the conversation:

"Susie, it's LD."

I knew exactly who it was because that voice is unmistakable.

"Hey, Lah, what's up?"

"I've got a part for you in this show I'm doing for HBO."

"What's the part?"

"Don't worry about it, it's just you. You just have to be yourself."

"Well, can I read the script?"

"There's no script. You play Jeff Garlin's wife. You'd be in three episodes. It's really low budget, there's no money. Will you do it?"

"Yeah, okay."

And so it began. I knew Larry's work was brilliant, Jeff was an old friend, it would probably be fun, and I didn't have to sign any contract because I was only making union day scale, so if I didn't like the project, I'd do three episodes and that would be it. What did I have to lose? I really had no idea what I was in for. As I write this, we are in the middle of shooting season seven. Who knew I'd end up on one of the funniest shows in the history of television?

A little background info—I first met Larry David somewhere in the mid-1980s in New York. We were doing stand-up and working the clubs. In those days there was a sense of community amongst the comics. There weren't that many of us, and we all knew one another. Larry and I weren't good friends, but we were colleagues and friendly (I hate the word *colleague,* it makes me sound like I'm a professor or someone testifying on behalf of a coworker). Every night, we'd all hang out at the bar at Catch A Rising Star, schmoozing while waiting to go onstage. In 1987 Larry was the head writer for a talk show Joy Behar was hosting on the Lifetime network, so I was thrown together with him a bit more. Larry was legendary. He never pandered to an audience or had that desperation to be liked that so many comics have. He had a deep sense of integrity about his comedy—not always the best recipe for success for a stand-up comic. He was eccentric but brilliant. All of the comics stood in the back of the room to watch when Larry was on because he was so funny and his material was completely original and something interesting would happen. There was no one else like him.

Then in 1990 Larry moved to Los Angeles to co-create and executive produce *Seinfeld,* and I don't think I saw him after that. The rest is history. In a decades-in-the-making instant, the comic's comic had become the voice of American comedy. This time, one of the good guys had won. Bitter and resentful are colors comics sometimes wear when one of our peers "makes it," but that wasn't the case when Larry David hit it big. I think all of the comics were happy for him. I know I was. I had such great respect for him and felt he deserved it. Also, it was kind of unexpected. If I had said to any random group of comedians standing at the bar at Catch in 1987 that Larry would be more successful than any of us, no one would have believed me. Not that he wasn't talented and a brilliant writer, it was just that he didn't seem to be that ambitious or that interested in making money, and he certainly wasn't mainstream. He was a totally unique comic voice. I thought it was great that with the success of *Seinfeld,* the rest of the world was exposed to, and appreciating, his comic genius.

As I said, I hadn't seen Larry in about nine years when I got his call, so I was a bit surprised to hear from him and have him offer me a part out of nowhere. It's great to be *given* a part. Auditioning is awful. It's a humiliating process, like a cavity search when you're first processed into prison (not that I've been in prison, but . . .) Here's how it works: You sit in a hall with a bunch of fellow desperados all trying out for the same part, until it's your turn and they call your name. You walk into a room devoid of furniture except for a long folding table covered with other people's 8 x 10s, and the casting director, and sometimes the producer or director are sitting behind it. You read a scene from the script with the casting director, who may or may not be able to act and who may or may not be the same sex as the character you're supposed to be in the scene with, and they put you on tape and the lighting is horrible so you know you look like shit and you want the part and they have the power to give it to you or not. Fun, huh? It's like putting your ego through a wood chipper. I'll bet half the shrinks in New York and L.A. built their beach houses in Nantucket on the psyches of struggling actors. Auditioning is a sucky situation. Nothing ever feels good about it. So when I'm offered something without having to audition, and the chance to work with someone for whom I have respect and admiration, I'm happy, even if it's not a big payday. Although, I will confess, I'm happier if it's a huge payday. Call me superficial. I later learned exactly how and why Larry thought of me for the part.

By 1999 I was frustrated with my career. I had been doing stand-up for sixteen years and had accomplished a lot, but I couldn't seem to "break through." I was making a decent living, appearing in clubs all over New York whenever and wherever I wanted. I had done lots of guest appearances on TV, had an HBO stand-up special, had paid my dues for sure and had become a good comic, but I was stuck. I remember time after time, coming offstage killing and thinking, *How much better do I have to be? How many more times do I have to kill?* I didn't know how to be any better than I was, but nothing was happening to bring me to that next level. No network was giving me a development deal, and in those days, they were giving them out to anyone with five minutes of material. I wasn't getting cast in anything. I also wasn't crazily ambitious. I wanted to make money and do good work and enjoy my life, but I didn't want to do anything that I didn't want to do, like move to Los Angeles as so many of my contemporaries had, which might have been the push my career needed. I liked the comfort of my life in New York. New York was home.

Luck, timing, and hard work are huge parts of a career in this business. My theory has always been to keep showing up and to keep doing the best work I could and sooner or later something would happen. In some ways it felt later rather than sooner, but the good part of that is that when I got lucky, I was good and ready. Show business is an industry with lots of people telling you no a lot of times, but you only need one yes to break your career, providing the yes comes from the right person. Sometimes it takes just one person to validate you. One person who's in a position of power to say to the world, "I think so-and-so is good and I'm going to give her a job." *Curb* put me on the map and gave me the public validation that helped crack the glass ceiling. Lots of people knew I was funny before I was on *Curb Your Enthusiasm,* but it was Larry David who gave me the opportunity. I must say, no man has ever used me so well.

It was fortuitous that in the fall of 1999, Larry saw me on *The Friars Club Roast of Jerry Stiller* on Comedy Central. He had just completed a one-hour special called *Larry David: Curb Your Enthusiasm* for HBO. Jeff Garlin, my soon-to-be television husband, was one of the executive producers of the special and played the part of Larry's manager. In the special, Jeff has a wife—whom he's cheating on, I might add—but she's never seen. When it came time to shoot the series for HBO based on the special, Larry needed to cast the part of Jeff's wife. Larry had written the character into three outlines (more about the outline process later), and there was one story

line in particular in which she had a pivotal role. In this episode, Jeff brings a Fresh Air Fund kid into the house against
his wife's wishes and the kid robs them blind. Jeff's wife then
goes into an angry tirade, screaming and yelling and cursing.
When Larry saw me on the Friars roast that fall, he was reminded of my existence and that I had a certain flair for certain language, which is what he was looking for. He called Jeff
and suggested me for the part of his wife. Jeff and I had been
buddies from way back in the New York stand-up days, and he
immediately thought it was a great idea.

It all so easily could have not happened if I hadn't done
that roast in the first place—and I almost hadn't. The Friars
Club was a perfect microcosm for the world of stand-up comedy, the ultimate "boys club." Women weren't even allowed
to join the Friars until 1988. And as for the roasts, they were
strictly stag affairs. They were absolutely filthy, and the men
felt that having women around would inhibit them in their
language. Wives weren't allowed—nor were girlfriends, mis-
tresses, paramours, or, quite frankly, anything with breasts,
except for Buddy Hackett. This went on for seventy years until
1983, when Phyllis Diller attended the roast disguised as a
man, wearing a suit and tie, beard, and moustache.

In 1988, the Friars finally decided to join the modern era
and allowed women to become members, but it wasn't until
1990 that a woman was even allowed to sit on the dais of a
roast. I joined the club in 1995. I was still a fledgling, and
many of the old regulars were still around—Henny Young-
man, Alan King, and Red Buttons; the guys I'd watched on *Ed
Sullivan* when I was a kid. Frank Sinatra was the abbott of the

club, which is the figurehead leader, and he signed my admission certificate, which is, to this day, pretty fucking cool. But if I thought the younger male comedians didn't think women were funny, that was nothing compared to these old guys. They were a completely different generation. Those guys took one look at me and thought, *This cute little girl can't possibly be funny.* And how do I know that? Because they said it to my face. Once I was on a show in Atlantic City that Alan King was hosting, and his intro for me was, "You know, in my day, all the funny women were ugly, but this broad is pretty *and* funny. Please welcome Susie Essman!" Was I supposed to take that as a compliment?

The Friars Club does a lot of charitable work and there's always a fund-raiser show going on at the club. All the performers work for free at these events. I did my share of them, and they were hard. These audiences had seen everyone and knew comedy. I made my bones and was on bills with a lot of comedy legends, which was intimidating, to say the least. Finally, in 1996, they trusted me enough and I got asked to do my first roast, The Friars Roast of Danny Aiello. The roasts are not held in the club, which is intimate and cozy, but in the Grand Ballroom of the New York Hilton, which is vast and cavernous and has a ridiculously high ceiling—acoustic death for comedy. Comedy needs a low ceiling so the laughs can hover and become contagious. In high-ceilinged rooms, the laughs just dissipate into the air. Even some of the best, most experienced comedians in the country die at these roasts. It's comic after comic hitting the same points about the roastee (we call them "roastees" rather than "honorees"; most people don't consider public humiliation an honor), and it's hard to be original. In order to do well at a roast you really need jokes. Good, solid jokes: set up, punch line, bang, bang, bang. I'm not that punchy. My style doesn't lend itself to that. But I made adjustments. The ability to work blue—even filthy— is also something of a requirement. But not just filthy, you needed to be filthy and smart, filthy and structurally sound, filthy and on point.

Language is one of the reasons why the roasts were stag only for so long. I had to show these boys that I could walk that fine line and keep up with them.

In 1999, the Friars were roasting Jerry Stiller. It was going to be televised on Comedy Central. Televising a roast kind of ruins the atmosphere for the same reason they excluded women all those years. It's supposed to be an inside thing, where it's safe to be outrageous and say and do whatever you want. Suddenly there's a camera there and the conceptual intimacy of the event is gone. It made a difficult job even more difficult. The Friars put together a list of comedians, including me, that they wanted on the show and submitted it to Comedy Central, but Comedy Central didn't want me. I'm not sure why, I don't think it was because they didn't think I was funny. Too old, too female, too Jewish, too who knows? I think they just didn't think I was their demographic. There's this demographic thing that the TV networks have, this ridiculous notion that eighteen-to-thirty-five-year-old boys only want to watch other eighteen-to-thirty-five-year-old boys. The networks are wrong. Funny is funny. I can't tell you how many college-aged boys approach me and tell me that they're obsessed with *Curb,* while we, the actors in it, are all old enough to be their parents and, sometimes, grandparents. Anyway, Comedy Central might have rejected me, but the Friars Club fought to have me on the show. Comedy Central gave in, I suppose figuring that they could edit me out. I worked with my friend Larry Amoros, a great comedy writer, and we put together a strong set for the roast. It took a lot of work. I put a lot of pressure on myself. In roasts, prep is everything. It's so stressful, especially if it's televised, and the room is difficult and filled with luminaries, so there's an intense vibe. You've got to go up there and know your stuff.

I got severe laryngitis a few days before. Emotional? Psychosomatic? Who knows? All I know is that I've never lost my voice like that before and I really thought that nothing at all would come out of my mouth when I got up there. Needless to say, my anxiety level was extreme. Fortunately, something did come out of my mouth, and it was funny. For my first line I knew I had to address the fact that I sounded like a croaking frog. I said, "I have to apologize, I'm very hoarse tonight. I have a sore throat. Jerry knows why. I know why. Enough said. It wasn't pretty." Then I turned to Alan King, who had taken over the role of Friars abbott after Frank Sinatra went to that great big nightclub in the sky, and said, "Alan, did you ever think you'd live so long that your prostate would be as big as your ego?" He roared. I had gotten the seal of approval by one of the last great old-timers. Touchdown. And the extra point was good.

That was the hard work part. The luck part was that Larry David saw it, was casting at the time, and offered me the role of Susie Greene. But it so easily could not have worked that way. He could have not seen it. Comedy Central could have not put me on. The Friars Club could have not fought for me. Nothing happens in isolation. I was fortunate, the stars were aligned, and I got the dream job of a lifetime.

MY FIRST day on the *Curb* set was a small scene. Jeff and I are at our house, and Jeff's parents (who are played by the wonderful Louis Nye and Mina Kolb) are there. All Larry told me was that I was Jeff's wife and I had a small child named Sammy, who, at that time, was a boy. (Sammy, who was never seen in the first season, has since become a girl because in season two Larry wrote an episode called "The Doll," my favorite episode of all time, and Sammy needed to be a daughter for the story line. In season three I was pregnant with our second child and was pushed off a balcony by Cheri Oteri, who was playing a deranged nanny. The fall was broken by twelve sponge cakes provided by Larry, and the pregnancy was saved. I have no idea, however, whatever happened to my baby. He/she was never referred to again in any future episodes.) Anyway, day one on the set we talked about what my name would be and settled on Susie. Larry told me what the scene was about and that at some point I'd be cued to interrupt the argument he was having with Jeff's parents and ask everyone to come upstairs to see how cute Sammy was. That was it.

I took one look at the house that we were using as a location (the first of several houses) and how it was decorated (it was all ultramodern), and the character just came to me. I decided that I was a devoted mother but also an interior decorator (part-time, of course), and believed that I had the greatest taste in the world. I didn't discuss that with anyone except Wendy Range-Rao, the wardrobe designer, to give her a sense of how I wanted to dress, outrageously but with complete confidence that I was on the cutting edge of high fashion. Kind of like the Russian women in Brighton Beach, Brooklyn. "Where am I going to get clothes like that?" she said. I told her to go to the Back Room at Loehmann's. Being a midwesterner, she had never heard of Loehmann's. We went on a field trip, and the Susie Greene look was born.

I flew home to New York and came back a month or so later to shoot the episode which would be my first shining, seminal, fuck-you moment. This particular scene takes place in our living room. Larry enters while I'm in the middle of screaming at Jeff because of the pilfering Fresh Air Fund kid. Larry told me a couple of pieces of information that were essential to the story line; I had to get them out at some point. Then he said something to the effect of, "I want you to rip Jeff a new asshole." *Okay,* I thought, *I can do that, I've been in a relationship before.* We did a few takes. Larry pulled me aside and told me not to hold back and really give it to Jeff. Another couple of takes. Then he pulled me aside again and said, "Make fun of Jeff's fatness."

"Larry, I can't do that. That's mean. Jeff's my friend."

Don't worry," he said. "He knows you're just acting and that it's not you really saying it to him. Trust me. Just go for it. Call him a fat fuck or something like that."

That was all it took. I was unleashed, and the genie never returned to the bottle. A couple of years later, Larry said to me, "Remember when I told you to make fun of Jeff's fat and to just go for it? Well, you *really* went for it."

Shooting that scene was so much fun. What other job could I possibly have where I can yell and scream and curse my head off and everyone loves me for it? At one point in the scene, Larry enters the room and I see him and say, "What the fuck are you doing here?" And he lost it. He got the giggles. That was the beginning of seven seasons of Larry laughing every time I yelled at him. Every single time, take after take after take. The man loves to be yelled at; he actually enjoys it. I think one of the reasons he's written me into the show all these years is that he takes such great pleasure in my screaming at him. He starts laughing before I even open my mouth. Just the anticipation alone is enough to send him into fits.

I knew from day one that this show was going to be special, but I didn't know it was going to last this long. It was such a slapdash operation. The budget was next to nothing. For example, the first two seasons, none of the actors had trailers or dressing rooms. No hair and makeup trailer. On top of that, Thomas Kolorek, our makeup artist, had to double as a hair person as well. It is kind of unheard of for a network show to have no place for the actors to change in privacy and hang out between takes. It was all catch-as-catch-can. We'd find a room somewhere, and that was that. There weren't even port-o-potties for the crew. I don't want to think of the improvising they had to do.

For seasons three and four, we finally had a trailer, but only one, and we all shared it. There was a bedroom to the left and a living room to the right and one bathroom for all of us, which wasn't always easy. At one point, Larry put up a sign—Bathroom Rules. It was like living in a dorm and Larry was the R.A. We'd change in the bedroom and hang out in the living room together between takes. Jeff was always walking around in his underwear. He enjoyed that. Everybody was in there together, whether it was Ben Stiller, or David Schwimmer, or Ted Danson, or the producers and directors. Believe me, other shows were not like this. I guarantee you that each and every one of those girls on *Sex and the City* had their own trailer from day one and a makeup trailer and a separate hairstylist. I imagine even the dogs and the extras had their own dressing rooms. But we didn't and didn't seem to even notice. In season five, we got trailers, but only because the producers were afraid that the union was going to come down on us and insist on it. I missed the communal trailer. It was fun; it didn't feel like we were doing a real show. We had no scripts, no lines to memorize, no trailer. It felt like camp or something.

After the first season I had no idea if the show was going to continue or if I was going to continue to be in it. I had no contract, and unfailingly at the end of each season, Larry announces, "I don't think I'm going to do another season. That's it." It's hard not knowing if and when we'll go back into production. I mean, I have a life and need to plan for things, but when it comes to *Curb,* it's Larry's world. I'm only living in it. About ten months after we wrapped season five, Larry called me and said, "Listen, I don't think we're going to come back, so if I were you, I'd take any job that comes along." I went into a bit of a depression. The thought of never putting those Susie Greene outfits on again caused me serious pain. And then six weeks later, he changed his mind and we were back on track and I once again got to scream and yell and kick him out of my house. I can't tell you the thrill I feel when I read an outline and there's some juicy action for me that invariably ends with me screaming, "Get the fuck out of my house, Larry!"

In seven seasons, Larry and I have never discussed who Susie Greene is. Not once. He instinctively got what I was doing and wrote my character into scenes, and I instinctively got what he wanted me to do. We've had a dialog of the unconscious for seven seasons. I never thought about who Susie Greene is, I just felt her. I know who she is inside and out, I know how she would react in any given situation and what her opinions are and how she feels, but I never consciously "created" her. I put on those wild outfits and just become her. (A moment to praise Christina Mongini, who has been the costume designer for *Curb* for the past three seasons. She has inspired me beyond belief with her understanding of the Susie Greene look. Putting together those outfits with Christina is one of the most fun parts of my job. However, the one phrase I've never said to her is "Can I keep this?")

I love Susie Greene, I love playing her, but I'm not her. People don't seem to get that. On an almost daily basis, on the sidewalks of New York, people stop and ask me to curse at them. I'm not kidding. I'll be standing at the produce section buying melons, and a woman will shove a cell phone in my face and in a pleading, begging voice, say, "It's my husband, call him a fat fuck please." This is what my life has become.

People beg me to curse at them. I'm not always in the mood. When I'm gracious and nice to them I can see visible disappointment in their faces. They want her, Susie Greene, and more often than not they'll start pushing me, egging me on, and finally to get rid of them I have to tell them to go fuck themselves and they walk away happy and I walk away feeling some kind of unexpected release.

On days when I have to do multiple takes of some screaming/yelling scene (and I always have to do multiple takes because Larry always ruins my best takes by giggling!), I go back to my hotel room and feel so relaxed. Like I had some primal scream therapy or something. It's good to get all that anger out and nobody gets hurt. But still, I'm not Susie Greene. There's some of me in her and plenty of her in me, although I think there's more of me in her than her in me, but I'm not her. It's called ACTING!

I do understand people's confusion. Lots of people on the show, like Richard Lewis, play themselves, but when Ted Danson is playing Ted Danson, he's not acting like himself, he's playing the character of Ted Danson. And Cheryl and Jeff and I have the same first names as our real-life selves, but we're playing characters. It's confusing. Just assume that none of us are who you think we are. Cheryl the person is so different from Cheryl the character. Cheryl Hines is fun loving and wacky and would laugh off half the things that annoy the pragmatic Cheryl David. Jeff Garlin is a man of principles and values. Jeff Greene is a big lug of a buffoon with no morality or ethics. Believe me, I would know, he's cheated on me (I mean Susie Greene) a million times.

And then there's Larry. I'd say that the question I'm asked more than any other is, "Is Larry like his character?" Sorry to disappoint, but the answer is no. That's not to say that they don't share some characteristics, because they do, but he is not that person. Larry says he aspires to be that guy. He likes that guy. That guy doesn't give in to any conventions or bullshit. He doesn't subscribe to the common niceties and behaviors that we all blindly follow, hypocritical though that may be. That guy is concerned with injustice and fairness. He says what so many of us are thinking but would never be caught dead saying. In real life, Larry may be thinking it too, but more often than not, I think, he keeps his mouth shut. He understands tact even if he doesn't like it.

For seven years, Larry was the show runner and executive producer of *Seinfeld,* one of the most successful shows ever. Do you know how much diplomacy it takes to do that? He couldn't go around just spewing whatever he was thinking. He was the boss, as he is on *Curb.* He has hundreds of people working for him and relying on him. We have a happy set, and that vibe comes from the top. I've been on unhappy sets. It's no fun. On *Curb,* we laugh all day. Off camera, I don't think a harsh word has ever passed between the four of us (Larry, Cheryl, Jeff, and me) in all these seasons. The fact that we actually like one another makes it possible for us to treat each other so horribly on-screen. The majority of our crew has been comprised of the same people for most of the show's seven seasons. You think they'd stick around and work for that schmuck Larry portrays on *Curb*? The real Larry is similar in some ways but oh, so much sweeter and more reasonable. Men come up to me all the time and say, "I'm exactly like Larry! I'm him!" I smile and act polite, but what I really want to say is, "No, you're nothing alike. You're an annoying neurotic accountant from Great Neck. Larry is a genius."

The second-most-asked question about *Curb* is, "Is the show really improvised?" Yes, it is. Sometimes people don't believe me. It is. I'm there. I know. That being said, it's not some free-for-all improv. It's structured and controlled. Larry writes ten outlines a season. He writes them himself but has a cadre of trusted advisors to bounce ideas off of. There's Alec Berg, Dave Mandel, and Jeff Schaffer, who also co-executive produce the show and direct a number of episodes. There's also Larry Charles and David Steinberg, who direct regularly. Jeff Garlin is an executive producer as well and has creative input. Usually all of the outlines are complete before we start shooting. They have to be, because each season has its own arc. For example, the arcs of season four were Larry starring in *The Producers* and Larry and Cheryl's tenth wedding anniversary. The arcs of season five were Larry trying to find out if he was adopted and Richard Lewis needing a kidney.

Each episode has an outline that's about seven pages long. The outline consists of each scene and what happens in each scene. It's all about the story. In every scene something happens that drives the story along. There's always information that needs to be conveyed in the scene. It's all right there in the outline. There's nothing superfluous, nothing that doesn't have some importance to the story. The only thing not in the outline is dialog—what the characters are going to say. Watch an episode. Pause after each scene and write a few lines about what happened—not what anyone said, but what happened—and you'll get it. As an actress it's a great way to work because it's all about intent. When I read the outline it's completely clear what's going on in the scene. I know who my character is and I know my relationship to the other characters, so the show really writes itself.

Sometimes we find the scene in the first take, but usually we do it five or six times before we figure out how to make it work. We try different things and play with it and keep some and leave out others. It's an extremely creative process. The greatest part about it for me as a comic is that I don't have to think about making it funny, which, in the end, makes it funnier. So often I'm given scripts for movies or other TV shows and I have to find ways to make them funny. On *Curb,* I have such faith in Larry that I know if he created the scene and it's meant to be funny, it'll be funny. I just have to be Susie Greene and be involved in the scene and it will work. I don't have to think about coming up with some witty line. It's not about that. It's a situation comedy in the truest sense of the term. For example, in one episode, Larry has to pretend to be an orthodox Jew to get in with the head of a kidney consortium, who is Orthodox. Larry wants to get a kidney donated for Richard Lewis so he doesn't have to give Lewis his own kidney. In order to impress the head of the consortium, Larry invites him and his daughter to a ski lodge for the weekend and Susie Greene has to pretend to be Larry's wife because Larry, of course, can't be married to the shiksa, Cheryl. Knowing the volatile history of Susie and Larry's relationship makes the situation hilarious before one word is even uttered. The scenes are laid out with such detail and packed with so much information and backstory that all I have to do is show up to the set and start to play. I read the outlines ahead of time, but it's really not essential. As a matter of fact, most of the guests on the show don't even get to see the outlines. They come to work and are told what the scene they're about to do is about. That way, they can't plan anything ahead of time. They won't be lying in bed the night before thinking of bad sitcom lines. You can't plan these scenes ahead of time. They have to play out organically and spontaneously.

The only time I ever thought of a line beforehand was in the restaurant opening episode in the finale of season three, where everyone is cursing to show solidarity with the chef suffering from Tourette's syndrome. It was necessary to come up with a line, because I wasn't in the scene reacting to what was happening. I was just walking in, cursing, and leaving, so I needed to make an impact. I couldn't rely on coming up with it in the moment as a reaction to the action in the scene. I was sitting in the group trailer thinking about it and thinking that Susie Greene likes alliterations like *fat fuck* and *four-eyed fuck.* And then I thought about the episode and what had gone down between Cheryl and myself and felt the righteous indignation that Susie Greene is so good at. I'm not in the episode until the very end, but I'm talked about throughout. Cheryl is annoyed with me because I canceled a lunch date with her claiming to have had a dental appointment. She then cancels lunch with me because she's stuck in a car wash (or so she says). When I show up at the restaurant, she has just yelled and cursed as part of the solidarity going on in the room. I think her rant is directed toward me and I respond in kind. Mmmmmmm, what to say, what to say? I didn't want to repeat any of my previous tirades, and then it just came to me. What's so great is that with that line and a few choice others I've been able to contribute to the pantheon of great TV character catchphrases. Think of all those memorable phrases that are indelibly etched in our psyches. Ralph Cramden's "To the moon, Alice." Ricky Ricardo's "Lucy, I'm home." Mary Richards's "Oh, Mister Grant." Or Archie Bunker's "Stifle it, Edith." And now, hopefully, someday, I'll be in the museum of broadcasting along with these other great TV characters with my own, "Fuck you, you car wash cunt! I had a dental appointment!"

I never could have imagined this show or this role. I never could have imagined that I'd become famous and beloved for telling people to go fuck themselves. That wasn't part of the plan, but there's an old Yiddish proverb that says, "You make plans, and God laughs."

We're both laughing at this one.

CHAPTER
16

FAT FEAR

I fear fat. F-A-T. FAT. Fatfatfatfat. I'm afraid of it, it scares the shit out of me, and I fear it's coming to get me. I don't like the way fat looks on me (I know, shocking), and I loathe the way it feels. When I gain even a small amount of weight I feel full, bloated, and lumbering, like some zoo animal that's just wolfed down a hundred pounds of lunch. I enjoy feeling light and breezy, like a cloud or an angel or a fluffy brioche. I like feeling as though I could just float away. But getting there is so hard.

My concern with fat has been heightened by the TV show *The Biggest Loser*. The cast members amaze me. I think they're so brave to go through what they're going through to lose weight, and to do it—wearing those horrifying midriff-revealing outfits—in front of tens of millions of viewers. They have to drop their defenses and egos before they can drop the weight. They're an inspiration to me and I admire them. They're addicts and I know how they struggle to break their addiction. I think it's harder to break an addiction to food than to drugs or alcohol, because we don't *need* alcohol (well, I need red wine, but besides that) or drugs to live, but we do need food. If we don't eat, we die; if we eat too much, we die. We can't live without it. We can't abstain or we'll abstain our way into the ground.

Everyone has an idea of how to lose weight, and nearly everyone, from Marie Osmond to Dr. Phil (neither of whom I'm inclined to listen to about too many things) has a book out about how to do it. Ultimately, we all know the routine. Bottom line, keep your fucking mouth shut. Don't use the refrigerator as a night-light. When there are leftovers, let them be left over for someone else. Eat less and exercise more. Burn more calories than you consume. A carrot has fewer calories and more nutrition than a cookie. Yeah, yeah, I get the concept. It's not that difficult to understand. It's difficult to execute!

I've never really been overweight. I'm down; I'm up but never so up that I'm a heart attack waiting to happen. Richard Simmons isn't knocking on my door waiting for me to burst into tears. Right now, I have this four pounds that I've been trying to get rid of for three years and I can't. It won't leave. My jeans are tight and I refuse to buy new ones. I refuse to give into the fact that this is who I am now. I know, for you folks reading this who have a lot more to lose than that, I'm annoying, and you're probably getting the urge to write me a "go fuck yourself" letter. I understand; all I'm saying is that I relate to how hard it is. In my own defense, you should remember that I work in television, and the camera "adds ten pounds," so four pounds for you is fourteen for me. Don't believe me? Did you know that in real life, Orson Welles only weighed 137 pounds?

I can diet for a week or two, but that's it. Beyond that I start feeling deprived and anxious, and I get restless and it's BORING! And if I can't do it, I don't know how other people can, because I actually love healthy food. I know, I know; I just got even more annoying, but what can I say? I really love vegetables. I even like them raw or steamed. I like yogurt, plain, no sugar or fruit added. I don't drink soda, just plain old water. I haven't eaten meat or chicken in twenty years. Besides French fries, which I hardly ever have and usually have them only when someone else orders them and I steal a few, I don't really like fried stuff, and on top of all that, I'm gluten intolerant so I *can't* eat cake and cookies and bread and pasta. So what the hell is this four pounds? And why the fuck can't I lose it? These folks on *Biggest Loser* are losing seven, eight, ten pounds an hour, and I can't get rid of this freaking four!

My friends keep giving me suggestions because I complain about these four pounds often. I graciously accept their help, but deep down I have no intention of doing anything they say. You know how there's always a friend who's an expert on everything? (My friends would say that friend is me, but whatever.) I have one friend who keeps telling me to cut out the cheese. Oy, what's the point? I already don't eat meat or chicken. A person needs protein, for God's sake. How much tofu can I consume? I've got to have something to look forward to. What's a girl to do?

Then they tell me to exercise more. More than what? I work out and I absolutely hate it! HATE IT! "But don't you feel better afterwards?" they ask. Of course I do. That's not the issue. I feel better after I eat chocolate too. It's the cardio that I really despise. I can get myself to do it every now and then, but ultimately it bores the shit out of me and I stop. Where's the conversation? Where's the distraction? And gyms are filthy, smelly things. Who the hell knows whose sweat you're consuming? Where is the joy in having to wipe down everything in sight with Purell?

Yet in spite of actually maintaining a pretty healthy diet, and working out a reasonable amount, still, nothing fits me. Thank heaven for Spanx. They are a godsend. If you don't know what they are, look it up online and buy them. They're control top to the nth degree. Not your grandmother's girdle. The only problem with them is the deception factor. Like the push-up bra. False advertising! When I was single I was afraid that I'd pour myself into an outfit and I'd look good but I'd be in there, you know, kind of unable to breathe or really move, and then I'd go on a date with someone new and then go home with them and take my clothes off and they would look at me naked and say, "You lied to me." As though I was a transvestite or something and instead of five extra pounds, I had a penis dangling between my legs.

That's just my insecurity, though, because the truth is, I don't trust guys who only like skinny girls. Any real man will tell you that there's nothing wrong with a little meat, and I don't buy into this Hollywood anorexic thing. I think those girls look like shit with their skinny collarbones sticking through their chests. So why, then, am I making such a big deal about the four measly pounds? Because it just plain and simple doesn't feel good. Everything feels tight. My blouses, my pants, my skin. Even my hair feels tight. I'm uncomfortable. I guess I'll just have to face the music and buy new jeans. I mean, I haven't reached the "Leisure World, can't cross my legs, need to ride a cart to go shopping, elastic waist band" stage yet, so I should be thankful for the little things. Oh fuck the little things! I want the big things! I want to lose these four goddamn pounds. That's a big thing to me!

If I can't lose the four pounds, how are these *Biggest Loser* people supposed to lose hundreds? It's such a daunting task, and yet they are committed and driven. I hold them in high esteem. But also, as I mentioned at the top of this chapter, in fear. Not of them, but of their fat. When they lose it, where does it go? It's matter, it exists, and they shed it in enormous amounts, hundreds of pounds, and what happens to it? Does it vaporize and go into the air, or does it morph into some other substance? It has to go somewhere. Are there just fat globules floating around in the atmosphere? That scares me. Can it glom onto me? It seems to be doing just that.

It's got to be out there. It can't just disappear. Maybe there are fat storage facilities somewhere, lipid lost and founds, or giant silos that hold all of this matter for future use. Maybe like compost, we could convert all of that extra fat into energy and cut down our dependence on foreign oil. How fabulous would that be? My head is spinning. Scientists take note: a new energy policy that would save lives and save money. And, on top of that, we'd all be svelte! What's not to like?

So, my weight-challenged friends, join me at the gym, let's all work out more, get on those treadmills, let's do that boring cardio! Let's save the planet! That's it. I'm doing it every day for at least twenty minutes. If I can contribute to saving the environment by losing four pounds, then I believe it's my civic duty. And though I can't save the earth all by myself, at least I'm compensating for the carton of ice cream I just threw out that will end up in a landfill somewhere in Staten Island.

CHAPTER
17

WHAT WOULD SUSIE SAY?

Curb Your Enthusiasm®/HBO®

S usie Greene is a character I play in the HBO show *Curb Your Enthusiasm.* She's been described in the press as foul-mouthed, venomous, vulgar, acid-tongued, vicious, suspicious, carping, volatile, a woman who has taken female cursing to longshoreman levels, and, most recently, in *Vanity Fair,* as "the Ionesco of invective." I don't agree with some of those descriptions. Yes, she's volatile and profane, but venomous and vicious? I don't think so. Suspicious? Well, yeah, but she *should* be, given the conduct of her fictitious cohorts, Larry and Jeff, who are always trying to pull one over on her. It's her screaming tirades that people remember, but it's her absolute comfort with her anger that makes her so appealing. Her shit-detecting abilities never fail her, and she's almost always right. The *New York Times* noted that Susie "hoards the moral authority of the show." I think that's accurate. Or as Susie Greene would say, "You're goddamn fucking right, she does."

Women come up to me all the time and tell me that Susie Greene is their hero. I love that. She's given women all across America permission to trust in the righteousness of their pent-up rage and let it loose. Susie Greene reacts from her gut and never questions her motivations. How liberating that must be. Why bother analyzing a situation and seeing all sides when she has experience and instinct on her side? Susie doesn't live in a state of doubt. She's completely clear and sure of herself. That's why she can dress the way she does. She's fiercely loyal to her kid, her husband, and even Larry sometimes. Believe me, if you're in trouble, you want Susie Greene on your side. She will fight to the death for you if she deems you worthy.

She experiences so many things as an indignity, but she doesn't see herself as angry. Let's not forget that more often than not, her anger is provoked and well earned. Larry steals her daughter's doll's head, Larry gets her daughter drunk, Jeff and Larry get them all kicked out of their country club, Larry insults her handmade sweatshirts, Larry is inappropriate with her dog, Larry tries on her bra, I could go on and on. Yeah, so maybe she has a short fuse, but she's not crazy. When you examine it, she has a reason for just about everything. Like when Larry refuses to take a tour of her new house. What kind of person doesn't take a tour of someone's new home? I've never heard of such a thing, and when Susie calls him a "freak of fucking nature," well, she's absolutely right!

Susie Greene and I both have no tolerance for bullshit, but we come from two different worlds and our opinions are colored by our distinct circumstances. For instance, while I'm happily married and content, her point of view is that of a bitter and disillusioned woman living in a miserable marriage. My advice might come from a healthier place, but cranky, nasty, and raging are so much funnier than cheerful and fulfilled. So when HBO asked me, during season five, to write an advice column in Susie Greene's voice for the *Curb Your Enthusiasm* website, I jumped at the opportunity. Real people wrote to Susie Greene with real problems, and she/I answered them on the website. She became the Ann Landers of angry. I don't know if people wrote in because they thought it was a real advice column or they just wanted to hear Mrs. Greene's unique take on things. I would never underestimate the naïveté of the public, but either way, I put on a leopard print outfit, got into character, and told them exactly what Susie would say.

Here are some excerpts from the column:

Dear Susie,

My husband gave me a beautiful diamond ring for our wedding anniversary. I decided to get it insured and was informed by the jeweler that the diamond was actually a piece of zircon. My husband claimed to have spent a lot of money when he bought it and explained that this gift was why he had to work so many late nights. Should I tell him that perhaps he has been ripped off?

Signed,

"Husband's Been Cheated," Kalamazoo, MI

Dear Husband's Been Cheated,

Now I've heard it all. WAKE THE F*** UP!!!!!!!!!! Working late to buy you a fake piece of shit? Either he's a total moron or you are. I hate to break it to you, honey, but the man is having an affair. Working late, my ass. If he doesn't have enough respect for you to buy you the real thing as a compensatory guilt gift, then you'd better hightail it out of there. Last time I suspected Jeff of cheating, it cost him big. I'm talking three carats pink cushion cut! For me, it was worth it. He can do whatever he wants as long as he knows how to pay for his indiscretions. Remember, a diamond is forever, but a man is only as good as his credit limit.

Susie

Dear Susie,

I've only been married six weeks and already my husband spends more time watching TV than talking to me. How can I get back the man I walked down the aisle with?

Signed

"The Honeymoon Is Over" Milwaukee, WI

Dear The Honeymoon Is Over,

You can't, and in the long run, you probably don't want to. Accept it and move on. That whole beginning romantic "in love" thing doesn't last. It's one of the great cosmic tricks that are played on us. Falling in love makes you deranged and clouds your judgment. Believe me, I was in love with Jeff once too, and then you wake up one day and look over and you're in bed with a fat f***. Consider yourself lucky if you can look at him over breakfast and not get nauseated. Cut your losses and get a hobby. I recommend rug weaving. Or you can always opt for the ultimate distraction and marital sex killer—have a kid.

Susie

Dear Susie,

I slept with my best friend's 18-year-old niece—what now?

Signed,

"The dog from Durango, CO"

Dear Dog from Durango,

Well, if I had any say in the matter, it would be jail! You're a sick pervert. Control yourself, for God's sake. Why do you old men always prey on these innocent young things? I think it's because a young girl won't know how bad you are in bed because she's got nothing to compare you to! You're just an insecure moron who doesn't have the balls to be with a real woman with real needs. Grow up and get counseling.

Susie

Dear Susie,

My 350+ pound friend wants to ride in my new sports car, but I don't think she fits and may be a bit too heavy for the car. What should I do?

Signed,

Shakey Shocks, Manhasset, NY

Dear Shakey Shocks,

Tell her. You'll be doing her a favor. Besides, do you think she doesn't know she's a fatty? Believe me, she's used to being discriminated against. My husband, Jeff, can barely fit into an SUV, let alone a sports car. And whose fault is that? Not mine. Not yours. She made her bed, so let her lie in it. At 350 plus that's probably all she can do anyway. Sorry if this sounds harsh, but remember, reality is your friend.

Susie

Dear Susie,

I've been struggling to break through as an actress for six months. Do you think a boob job would help or hurt?

Signed,

"Anna Nicole with an A-cup," Ann Arbor, MI

Dear Anna Nicole with an A-cup,

Get one, it will help. My husband is a very prominent man in the entertainment world and all he and his successful show biz cronies do is stare at women's boobs. I'd go so far as to say that they're obsessed with them. I happen to have been genetically blessed with an attractive bustline. The first time I met Jeff I caught him eyeing my décolletage and I knew I had him right where I wanted him. Flash a little boob and they're putty in your hands. If they're dumb enough to think a plastic ball is a turn-on, then beat them at their own game. They're all a bunch of frigging idiots anyway, so use it.

Susie

Dear Susie,

My libido is through the roof and my husband thinks I'm crazy.

Signed,

Samantha, Syracuse, NY

Dear Samantha,

If your husband is anything like my husband, then you're certifiable. But seriously, you are probably going through some kind of hormonal fluctuation. Calm down and don't make a spectacle of yourself. Get a prescription for Prozac or Zoloft or one of the popular antidepressants out there. They diminish your libido and cheer you up all at once. It's a win-win! Volunteer for sex, and you erode your power base. Never forget that one of the keys to a great partnership is to always make him beg for it.

Susie

Dear Susie,

I'd like to tell my husband more about what makes me happy in bed, but I'm extremely shy (I don't even look at myself when I'm changing!) Any suggestions on how to break the ice?

Signed,

"Shy and Deprived," Queens, NY

Dear Shy and Deprived,

Go shopping at Loehmann's, where you'll be forced to use the communal dressing room. Practice by telling the woman trying to fit a size 12 body into a size 6 dress how she really looks. You'll feel empowered (and you'll get some good buys too)!

Susie

Dear Susie,

I'm 63 and I just started dating a 23-year-old man. My friends think he must be after my money. What do you think?

Signed,

"Still Got It," Naples, Florida

Dear Still Got It,

Well of course he's after your money. What kind of stupid question is that? But who cares!

As long as you're getting it from a 23-year-old, enjoy yourself. You're using him too, aren't you? He must bore the crap out of you when you're not in bed. He's probably good for about an hour and then he gets out of bed and wants to watch cartoons and asks for a nice cold glass of Bosco. Just keep it in perspective and don't

227

write him into the will. Oh, and if he calls you Mommy, kick him the hell out. That's just sick.

Susie

Dear Susie,

Last year I was married and one of my friends attended my wedding and didn't give me a gift. She's getting married next month—should I give her a gift or not?

Signed,

"Too rude," Springfield, MA

Dear Too Rude,

Well, the mature, reasonable part of me says that two wrongs don't make a right and you don't have to stoop to their level and take the high road, etc., but my gut tells me that these lowlifes don't deserve a damn thing. Marriage is a sacred thing, and if these people can't acknowledge the sacrifice you're making, then screw them. Marriage is not easy, but it's a necessary evil and something we all must endure. It's only right that you should get gifts that will help to ease the pain.

Susie

Dear Susie,

I work with a guy who is long-winded and no one can have a conversation with a coworker without him butting in with, "Well that's just it..." and he repeats what the person had stated succinctly and then adds his own thoughts. I tend to walk away from a conversation when he comes around because I am sick

of the inevitable. Should I stick with this or should I call him out
on the matter?
Signed,
"Dealing with the elaborator," Winnipeg, MB

Dear Dealing with the Elaborator,
Your instinct to walk away is correct and you should get everyone
in the office to do the same. These insufferable blowhards never
hear themselves and are way too full of their own self-importance
to stop for a moment and look within. Calling him out on the matter
will be futile. He won't even get the hint if everyone walks away.
He'll find some excuse to protect his own ego and make himself the
victim. There is no greater sin than to be aggressively boring. If he
ends up with no one to talk to, tough shit. You reap what you sow.
Susie

Dear Susie,
Two coworkers at my job are having an affair that everyone
knows about. The floozy lives in my neighborhood and I run
into her with her family at the supermarket all the time. I feel
guilty as hell that I know and feel her husband should get a hint.
Do you think someone should "inadvertently" spill the beans?
Signed,
"Worried Worker," Westbury, NY

Dear Worried Worker,
Keep your mouth shut. Ever hear of killing the messenger? Besides, things are not always what they seem. For all you know, he's
glad she's not bothering him. I know I feel that way many times.

Or maybe he's cheating on her as well. Who knows? The bottom line is, it's none of your business and why are you so invested in their marriage anyway? Maybe it's time for you to look within. Perhaps you feel guilty about your own wandering eye? Hmmmmm?

Susie

Dear Susie,

My male pattern baldness is really starting to assert itself. What's the answer? Comb-over? Plugs? Pharmaceuticals? Toupee? Or let nature run its course?

Signed,

"Follically Challenged," Maplewood, NJ

Dear Follically Challenged,

The fact that you would even consider a comb-over or toupee is deeply disturbing. Look around you and see how ridiculous these men look. Two words—fooling no one! Plugs may be an option if done well, but I've seen too many men who make me want to take a magic marker and play connect the dots on their heads. There's nothing wrong with baldness if you've got the face for it. Look at Sean Connery. (Of course the odds are you don't look like him.) Even so, I'd let nature run its course. Women don't care about it as much as you think. Secretly, we actually like it because we know how scared you men become at the first sign of baldness. It gives us pleasure to see you suffer and obsess over your looks in middle age because we've been doing it since we were twelve! Oh, and if you're lucky enough to be a black man, then just shave your head. You'll look supercool. White men who try it look like serial killers.

Susie

Dear Susie,

I work in very close quarters with my boss, who frequently rides her bike to work. Suffice it to say that my coworkers and I are "this close" to wearing hazmat gear to work just to protect ourselves from her insidious body odor. Is there a tactful way to let her know that she, uh, reeks?

Signed,

The "Give us Arrid X-tra Dry" Armpit Army

Dear Armpit Army,

There is no tactful way to tell her. There never is. Can't she smell herself? That's what I never understand with these smelly types. I usually opt for honesty, but in this case I think you have to go the cowardly route because she's your boss. Subtle hints like leaving a can of deodorant on her desk are not going to work. You've got to leave an anonymous note and tell her quite frankly that she stinks and is alienating her employees. Sure, she'll be mortified, but in the long run, you're doing her a favor. To me, there is nothing more loving you can say to a friend than "you need a mint."

Susie

Dear Susie,

I love my wife and we've been married for about three years. I still love her but I am attracted to and want to be with other women. I am only 34 years old and I feel trapped sometimes. How can I control my wanting to be with other women? Or should I discuss it with her?

Signed,

Brent, Washington, DC

Dear Brent,

Oh, grow the f*** up! What do you think, you're the only person who has ever had a wandering eye? Have you ever seen my husband? If you think I'm not looking at all these hunks running around parking cars in Hollywood, you're mistaken. We all feel trapped. That's what marriage is. That's why we did it in the first place. Get used to suffering and learn to enjoy it.

Susie

Dear Susie,

I am single and started meeting men on the internet. I met this very interesting, intellectual and sexy guy. He said that I was his soul mate, his dream girl, the love of his life. The next day, he dumped me with a text message on my cell phone. Besides being so cowardly, don't you think that this is an improper use of technology?

Signed,

Janine, Los Angeles, CA

Dear Janine,

You live by the sword, you die by the sword. Men are cowards no matter how you meet them. You're lucky you even got a text message. How many times have I heard from my girlfriends that the guy never called again? Your biggest mistake was believing anything he said in the first place. They lie all the time. It's their mission on this earth. The sooner you understand that, the happier you'll be. Realize that they are slaves to their biological impulses and assume the worst, and you'll never be disappointed. On the positive side, if men didn't try to relentlessly get women in bed, then where would we be? Certainly not shopping at Neimans, and oh, the pleasures we'd be missing out on.

Susie

Dear Susie,

I was out of town one weekend and my best friend and husband slept together. What should I do? Right now I am not speaking to her and I am still with my husband. Me and my best friend have mutual friends and it is very awkward for our friends when either of our names are brought up. Should I give her a second chance at a friendship? We were very close but it still hurts. Please help.

Signed,

"Stabbed in the Back," Indiana

Dear Stabbed in the Back,

Listen to me carefully. YOUR HUSBAND SLEPT WITH YOUR BEST FRIEND!!!!! Get the f*** rid of both of them immediately and then get yourself some self-esteem. Look, Stabbed, I'm not saying that husbands never cheat. Of course they do, they're men. But he should have had the decency to go outside of your social circle. You don't shit where you eat, and as far as I can tell, they've both shit on you. Time to flush them into the sewer, which is where they belong anyway.

Susie

Dear Susie,

I am about to become engaged to a wonderful woman. We are both previously married and now divorced. She wants an engagement ring with a diamond bigger than the one I gave my first wife. However, once we get married, we are going to want to buy a house and furnish it and I am afraid that money is going to be tight. I was trying to be practical so I suggested that we use the diamond that her first husband gave her (which is huge) and just have it reset. Now she is furious with me. Do you think I'm being too cheap?

Signed,

"Just Being Practical," Washington, DC

Dear Just Being Practical,

"Just being stupid and insensitive" would be more accurate! What the hell is the matter with you? Use the ex-husband's diamond?! Are you crazy?! I've never heard of such an insulting thing in my whole life. Even Jeff would be smarter than that. She's right to want a diamond bigger than the one you gave your ex to prove your love and devotion to her. How else will she know that you love her more than the ex? If you had a brain in your head, you would have suggested selling her ex's diamond to pay for your new house. Of course she should say no to that as well because I'm sure she earned that one fair and square, but at least you would have looked like less of an insensitive lout. I don't care if you have to beg, borrow, or steal, but the only way for you to keep your relationship intact is to now go out and get her an even bigger diamond than she wanted in the first place. You put your foot in your big mouth, now put your hand in your thin wallet. If you don't, she has every right to call off the engagement. As a matter of fact, I would encourage it.

Susie

Dear Susie,

My husband seems inappropriately attached to our dog Butch. He's always touching him. Am I overreacting?

"Wife of a Dog Lover"

Dear Wife of a Dog Lover,

No. Believe me, I've seen this scenario before. A friend of my husband's, I don't want to mention any names, became aroused from petting my dog Oscar. It's disgusting. These poor dogs are just innocent victims of these perverts. If you want to keep the husband, then get rid of the dog, but I suggest keeping the dog and dumping the man. Next you'll find him loitering at dog runs begging for some tail. No good can come from this!

Susie

Dear Susie,

Do you think it's right that while I was away my domestic partner went and helped an attorney get a hotel room so he could have sex with another woman (he's married) and charge it to his charge card and doesn't feel he did anything wrong. I say he's a prick and I only found out because he was stupid to hide the bill and of course I found it. When confronted he said he helped out an attorney who lost his wallet. What a bullshit story ... I of course kept after him and accused him that he was the one who betrayed me ... and then finally he confessed he helped a friend out. My question to you is—would you believe him ... because I don't ...

Signed

Gladys, Brooklyn, NY

Dear Gladys,

Do you even have to ask? He's not your "domestic partner," he's an asshole. He's also a liar, and a really bad one, to boot. And have I mentioned stupid? First rule of thumb when cheating, pay in cash. The fact that he left a paper trail of his indiscretion and then a lame lie like a lost wallet to cover is just too pathetic and makes me think that he wanted to get caught. Now you have two choices. Either you can leave him, or you can let him stay and make him pay for it and suffer. If I were you, I'd choose the latter. This man is obviously of marginal intelligence and you can probably manipulate him to get everything you want and need. Remember, never forgive. You've got something on him, now use it. This may all be a blessing in disguise.

Susie

Dear Susie,

My roommate has been asking me to hot-tub in the nude, and now she says she wants to give me a massage. Do you think she's gay?

Signed,

"Perplexed," San Antonio, Texas

Dear Perplexed,

Yes.

Susie

ABOUT THE AUTHOR

Susie Essman has played the sassy Susie Greene for all seven seasons of the critically acclaimed HBO comedy series *Curb Your Enthusiasm.* Her hilarious bouts of withering sarcasm and uninhibited insults have become her character's trademark and her streetwise vernacular is perfectly suited for her life in Manhattan, where she has been a veteran of the world of stand-up comedy for twenty-five years. Essman has appeared on numerous television shows and has graced several films, most recently co-starring with John Travolta as the voice of Mittens the Cat in the Disney animated film *Bolt.* She divides her time between New York City and upstate New York, where she lives with her husband, four stepchildren, and two dogs.